Advanced Placement
ECONOMICS

Macroeconomics: Student Activities
3rd edition

John S. Morton

Rae Jean B. Goodman

This publication was made possible through funding by

The Goldman Sachs Foundation

COUNCIL FOR
**Economic
Education**
Council For Economic Education

Authors

Authors

John S. Morton is Vice President for Program Development at the National Council on Economic Education. Previously, he was a high school economics teacher, director of the Governors State University Center for Economic Education and president of the Arizona Council on Economic Education.

Rae Jean B. Goodman, Director of Teaching and Learning and Professor of Economics, has had more than 30 years of teaching and administrative experience at the U.S. Naval Academy. She served as a table leader and the Chief Faculty Consultant for the Advanced Placement Economics Examinations from 1989 until 1997.

Editor

Melinda Patterson Grenier was a reporter, deputy bureau chief and bureau chief at the print and online Wall Street Journal. A former teacher, she was also the founding editor and publisher of The Wall Street Journal Classroom Edition, an award-winning educational program for high school economics teachers and students.

Artist

Susan A. Mills received her bachelor of fine arts degree in art from the University of Connecticut. She is employed as a Test Publishing Coordinator at Educational Testing Service in Princeton, N.J.

Project Director

Claire Melican is Vice President for Program Administration at the National Council on Economic Education. In addition to teaching economics at the college level, Claire has worked at the Educational Testing Service where she was instrumental in the development and implementation of the Advanced Placement Examinations in Economics until 2000.

ISBN: 978-1-56183-567-6

5 4 3

Macroeconomics | Contents

Unit 4   Money, Monetary Policy and Economic Stability

Advanced Placement Economics Macroeconomics: Student Activities © Council For Economic Education, New York, N.Y.

Macroeconomics | Unit 1

Basic Economic Concepts

■ Scarcity exists because we have limited resources and unlimited wants. No society has ever had enough resources to produce all the goods and services its members wanted.

■ Because of scarcity, all decisions involve costs.

■ Opportunity cost is the forgone benefit of the next best alternative when resources are used for one purpose rather than another.

■ A production possibilities curve graphically illustrates scarcity, choices and opportunity costs.

■ The slope of a production possibilities curve shows the opportunity cost of producing one more unit of one good in terms of the amount of the other good that must be given up.

■ The law of comparative advantage shows how everyone can gain through trade by specializing in producing the good or service with the lowest opportunity cost.

■ In a market system, resources are allocated in response to relative prices.

■ A demand curve shows all the prices and quantities at which consumers are willing and able to purchase a good or service. The law of demand states that consumers will want to buy more at a lower price and less at a higher price.

■ There is a difference between a change in demand and a change in quantity demanded. A change in quantity demanded is a movement along the demand curve and can be caused only by a change in the price of the good or service. At a lower price, a larger quantity is demanded. A change in demand is a shift in the curve whereby more or less is demanded at every price. Changes in prefer-ences, incomes, expectations, population, or the prices of complementary or substitute goods will cause a change in demand.

■ A supply curve shows all the prices and quantities at which producers are willing and able to sell a good or service. Producers want to sell more at a higher price and less at a lower price.

■ There is a difference between a change in supply and a change in quantity supplied. A change in quantity supplied is a movement along the supply curve and can be caused only by a change in the price of the good or service. At a lower price, a smaller quantity is supplied. A change in supply is a shift of the curve whereby more or less is supplied at every price. A change in technology, in pro-duction costs or in the number of sellers (firms) will cause a change in supply.

■ In competitive markets, supply and demand schedules are the sum of many individual decisions to sell and to buy. The interaction of supply and demand determines the price and quantity that will clear the market. The price where the quantity supplied and quan-tity demanded are equal is called the equilib-rium or market-clearing price.

■ Equilibrium prices and quantities are deter-mined as follows: At a price higher than equilibrium, there is a surplus and pressure on sellers to lower their prices. At a price lower than equilibrium, there is a shortage and pressure on buyers to offer higher prices.

■ In a market economy, prices provide informa-tion, allocate resources and act as rationing devices. It is important to know how to illus-trate a wide range of situations with supply and demand graphs.

■ Price elasticity of demand refers to how much the quantity demanded changes in relation to a given change in price. If the percentage change in quantity demanded is greater than the percentage change in price, the demand for the good is considered elastic. If the percentage change in quantity demanded is less than the percentage change in price, the demand for the good is considered inelastic. If the percentage change in price is equal to the percentage change in quantity demanded, the demand for the good is considered unit elastic.

Scarcity, Opportunity Cost and Production Possibilities Curves

Scarcity necessitates choice. Consuming or producing more of one commodity or service means consuming or producing less of something else. The opportunity cost of using scarce resources for one commodity or service instead of something else is often represented in graphical form as a *production possibilities curve.*

Part A

Use Figures 1.1 and 1.2 to answer Questions 1 and 2. Fill in the answer blanks, or underline the correct answer in parentheses.

 Figure 1.1

Production Possibilities Curve 1

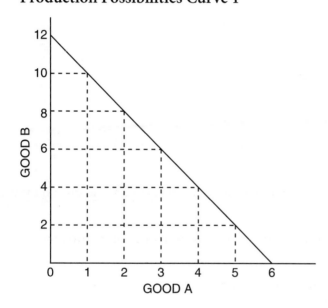

1. If the economy represented by Figure 1.1 is presently producing 12 units of Good B and zero units of Good A:

   (A) The opportunity cost of increasing production of Good A from zero units to one unit is the loss of _____ unit(s) of Good B.

   (B) The opportunity cost of increasing production of Good A from one unit to two units is the loss of _____ unit(s) of Good B.

   (C) The opportunity cost of increasing production of Good A from two units to three units is the loss of _____ unit(s) of Good B.

   (D) This is an example of (*constant / increasing / decreasing / zero*) opportunity cost per unit for Good A.

✳ Figure 1.2
Production Possibilities Curve 2

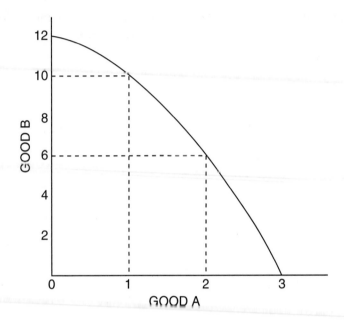

2. If the economy represented in Figure 1.2 is presently producing 12 units of Good B and zero units of Good A:

   (A) The opportunity cost of increasing production of Good A from zero units to one unit is the loss of _____ unit(s) of Good B.

   (B) The opportunity cost of increasing production of Good A from one unit to two units is the loss of _____ unit(s) of Good B.

   (C) The opportunity cost of increasing production of Good A from two units to three units is the loss of _____ unit(s) of Good B.

   (D) This is an example of (*constant / increasing / decreasing / zero*) opportunity cost per unit for Good A.

Part B

Use the axes in Figures 1.3 and 1.4 to draw the type of curve that illustrates the label above each axis.

Figure 1.3

Production Possibilities Curve 3

Increasing opportunity cost per unit of Good B

Figure 1.4

Production Possibilities Curve 4

Constant opportunity cost per unit of Good B

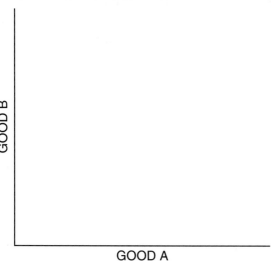

Part C

Use Figure 1.5 to answer the next five questions. Each question starts with Curve BB' as a country's production possibilities curve.

 Figure 1.5

Production Possibilities Curve: Capital Goods and Consumer Goods

3. Suppose there is a major technological breakthrough in the consumer-goods industry, and the new technology is widely adopted. Which curve in the diagram would represent the new production possibilities curve? (Indicate the curve you choose with two letters.) _____

4. Suppose a new government comes into power and imposes a significant tax on the use of automated machinery and modern production techniques in all industries. Which curve in the diagram would represent the new production possibilities curve? (Indicate the curve you choose with two letters.) _____

5. Suppose massive new sources of oil and coal are found within the economy, and there are major technological innovations in both industries. Which curve in the diagram would represent the new production possibilities curve? (Indicate the curve you choose with two letters.) _____

6. If BB' represents a country's current production possibilities curve, what can you say about a point like X? (Write a brief statement.)

7. If BB' represents a country's current production possibilities curve, what can you say about a point like Y? (Write a brief statement.)

Opportunity Cost and Comparative Advantage

People who don't know much about economics often dismiss economics as being little more than cost/benefit analysis. While it is true that this is a very important concept, economics is not that simple. In fact, one of the most difficult concepts in economics is understanding the opportunity cost of choosing a particular action.

We have seen that economic entities such as countries often face *increasing* opportunity costs as they try to increase production. For instance, when a country finds itself at war and needs to increase its production of armaments, at first it finds that increasing military production comes at a relatively low opportunity cost, as the first factories converted to military use are generally well-suited for such an event.

As the war goes on, however, we see factories that are not at all well-suited to producing weapons being converted to military use, at a very high opportunity cost. Little is added to the output of armaments, and a great deal is sacrificed in terms of consumer goods.

The notion of increasing opportunity costs is manifested in a production possibilities curve that is concave towards the origin. In Figure 2.1, we can see that as we increase the production of military goods, each additional unit of output costs more in terms of civilian goods. When the government initially

✳ Figure 2.1
Production Possibilities Curve: Military and Civilian Goods

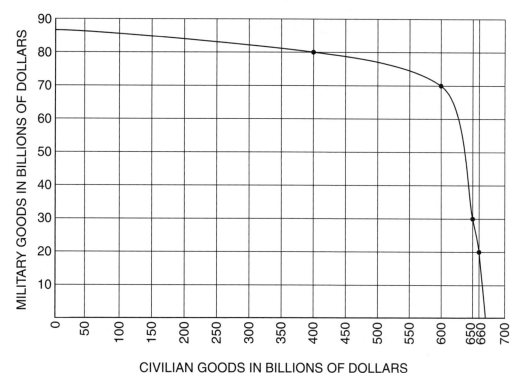

Activity written by Ike Brannon, Joint Economic Committee, U.S. Senate, Washington, D.C.

increases the output of military goods from $20 billion to $30 billion, the opportunity cost (in terms of civilian goods forgone) is small: only $10 billion of military goods ($660 billion minus $650 billion).

However, when the country is already producing a lot of military goods and wants to produce even more, the cost is much higher. If the country is producing $70 billion and wants to produce $80 billion, the opportunity cost is now $200 billion, or $600 billion minus $400 billion.

Opportunity cost also explains the incredible amount of trade that goes on among individuals, firms and countries. Today, of course, few of us produce our own goods and services; we rely on others to do this while we use our time earning money at a job. Instead of making our goods, we buy them. Computer manufacturers actually produce few of their own parts, but instead buy parts from suppliers.

Countries tend to specialize in the production of goods and services as well; for instance, there aren't any firms in the United States currently making television sets, and we make very few consumer electronics of any sort. Instead, our businesses concentrate on making other goods and services, and we import the televisions we need.

As we will see, we benefit from trade with other countries even if we are better at producing *everything* than the other country. Trade will benefit both countries as long as we each specialize in doing the task for which we have a lower opportunity cost. This is called *comparative advantage*.

Part A: Examples

Let's begin with a simple example. One summer two friends, Ty and Jessica, each started a business, making money by providing lawn-care services. Although they earned decent money working alone, they wondered if they could make more money by working together. The table below shows how many minutes it takes for each to complete the two tasks involved in doing one lawn: mowing and trimming, which includes the sweeping, edging and cleanup.

	Mow	Trim
Ty	60 minutes	40 minutes
Jessica	75 minutes	90 minutes

Someone who can do an activity using fewer resources is said to have an *absolute advantage*. Ty has an absolute advantage at both activities. Does this mean he should continue working alone?

If your instinct is to say that Ty should not partner with Jessica, you are wrong, but you are in good company: Adam Smith, whom many regard as the founder of modern economics, thought the same thing. It wasn't until David Ricardo came along in the early 1800s that people realized specialization and trade *can* benefit everyone *even if one of the parties has an absolute advantage at both activities!*

If Ty and Jessica are going to specialize, who should do what? Now, absolute advantage does not tell us anything, since Ty is better at both things. Instead, we have to look at *comparative advantage*.

We say someone has a comparative advantage at a task if this person can do the task at a *lower opportunity cost* than the other person.

Here, the opportunity cost of Ty mowing a lawn is how much of a lawn he could have trimmed in the same time. In this case, Ty could have used the 60 minutes it takes him to mow one lawn and he could have trimmed $1^1/_2$ lawns, or $^3/_2$ lawns.

For Jessica, the opportunity cost of mowing one lawn is what she could have trimmed during the 75 minutes she needed to mow that lawn. Jessica could have trimmed only $5/6$ (or $75/90$) of a lawn. Thus, we can see that Jessica has a comparative advantage in mowing lawns because Jessica's opportunity cost of mowing a lawn is lower than Ty's: Five-sixths of a lawn trimmed is less than $3/2$ lawns trimmed.

Now, we can calculate their opportunity cost to *trim* lawns. It takes Ty 40 minutes to trim one lawn, and with these 40 minutes he could instead have mowed $2/3$ of a lawn (or $40/60$). For Jessica, instead of using 90 minutes to trim one lawn, she could have spent these 90 minutes mowing one lawn and $1/5$ of another lawn ($90/75$). Thus, Ty has a comparative advantage in trimming lawns. The table below shows the relative opportunity costs.

	Opportunity cost of mowing one lawn	Opportunity cost of trimming one lawn
Ty	$3/2$ lawn trimmed	$2/3$ lawn mowed
Jessica	$5/6$ lawn trimmed	$6/5$ lawn mowed

Notice two things about our calculation of opportunity cost: First, Ty's opportunity cost of mowing one lawn ($3/2$ lawns trimmed) is the reciprocal of his opportunity cost of trimming one lawn ($2/3$). This will always be true, so in this example we did twice as much math as we would normally have to.

Second, notice that each person has a comparative advantage in precisely one activity. Unless a person is equally able at both activities, this will always be true as well.

Next, let's see whether this specialization actually increases their productivity. Before specializing, it would take Jessica 165 minutes (90 + 75) to mow and trim one lawn and Ty 100 minutes (60 + 40) to mow and trim one lawn, for a total of 265 minutes. If Jessica mows two lawns and Ty trims two lawns, then the total time needed to do two lawns would be 150 (75 x 2) + 80 (40 x 2) minutes or 230 minutes.

Thus, they save 35 minutes, or 13 percent of the total time necessary to do the lawns without specializing. Together, they can do more lawns in a week, and they can split the additional income so both are richer.

Let's look at one more example. Here, we will express the relative productivity of each person not in the number of minutes they need to do the activity but instead in *how many activities they can do in an hour*.

A few years ago Mark and Doreen were earning extra money installing car stereos for a local electronics store when they decided to go into business for themselves. After they rented a garage, they had to decide who should do what activity. The table below describes their productivity in the number of stereos and speakers installed per hour.

	Mark	Doreen
Radios installed	6	10
Speakers installed	2	5

The table below contains the breakdown of the opportunity cost for each person to do each activity.

	Mark	Doreen
Installing 1 radio	$1/3$ speaker	$1/2$ speaker
Installing 1 speaker	3 radios	2 radios

Mark has the comparative advantage in installing radios, and Doreen has the comparative advantage in installing speakers. By specializing, their total output increases.

Part B: Questions

1. What is the difference between comparative advantage and absolute advantage?

2. You're given the following information about a newlywed couple and the time it takes each of them to do two different chores: vacuuming a room or washing a load of dishes.

	Mike	Debbie
Vacuum a room	60 minutes	45 minutes
Wash a load of dishes	30 minutes	45 minutes

(A) What is Mike's opportunity cost of vacuuming in terms of washing dishes?

(B) What is Mike's opportunity cost of washing dishes in terms of vacuuming?

(C) What is Debbie's opportunity cost of vacuuming in terms of washing dishes?

(D) What is Debbie's opportunity cost of washing dishes in terms of vacuuming?

(E) Who has the *absolute* advantage in vacuuming? _____

(F) Who has the *absolute* advantage in washing dishes? _____

(G) Who has the *comparative* advantage in vacuuming? _____

(H) Who has the *comparative* advantage in washing dishes? _____

(I) Who should do which chore and why? Base your answer only on the information above and on comparative advantage considerations.

3. Now, you're given the following information about Andy and Hannah and the time it takes each of them to clean an office and clean a jail cell:

	Andy	Hannah
Cleaning offices	60 minutes	20 minutes
Cleaning jail cells	30 minutes	15 minutes

(A) What is Andy's opportunity cost of cleaning offices in terms of cleaning jail cells?

(B) What is Hannah's opportunity cost of cleaning offices in terms of cleaning jail cells?

(C) What is Andy's opportunity cost of cleaning jail cells in terms of cleaning offices?

(D) What is Hannah's opportunity cost of cleaning jail cells in terms of cleaning offices?

(E) Who has the *absolute* advantage in cleaning offices? _____

(F) Who has the *absolute* advantage in cleaning jail cells? _____

(G) Who has the *comparative* advantage in cleaning offices? _____

(H) Who has the *comparative* advantage in cleaning jail cells? _____

(I) Who should do which chore and why? Base your answer only on the information above and on comparative advantage considerations.

4. Consider the following two countries. Assume they produce only these two goods. *Note that productivity is now measured in how many goods can be produced per hour*, the opposite of how we measured it in Questions 2 and 3.

	United States	Japan
Cars	12	10
Computers	4	6

(A) What is the United States' opportunity cost of making cars?

(B) What is Japan's opportunity cost of making cars?

(C) What is the United States' opportunity cost of making computers?

(D) What is Japan's opportunity cost of making computers?

(E) Which country has the *absolute* advantage in cars? _____

(F) Which country has the *absolute* advantage in computers? _____

(G) Which country has the *comparative* advantage in cars? _____

(H) Which country has the *comparative* advantage in computers? _____

(I) Which country should produce which good and why? Base your answer only on the information above and on comparative advantage considerations.

5. Use the law of comparative advantage to explain why self-sufficiency leads to a lower standard of living.

Demand Curves, Movements Along Demand Curves and Shifts in Demand Curves

Part A

Figure 3.1 shows the market demand for a hypothetical product: Greebes. Study the data, and plot the demand for Greebes on the axes in Figure 3.2. Label the demand curve D, and answer the questions that follow. Write the correct answer in the answer blanks or underline the correct words in parentheses.

 Figure 3.1
Demand for Greebes

Price ($ per Greebe)	Quantity Demanded (millions of Greebes)
$.10	350
.15	300
.20	250
.25	200
.30	150
.35	100
.40	50

 Figure 3.2
Demand for Greebes

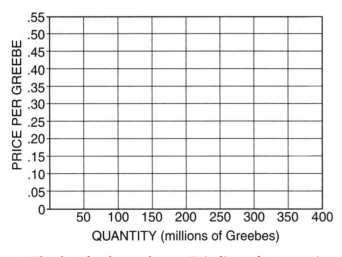

1. The data for demand curve D indicate that at a price of $0.30 per Greebe, buyers would be willing to buy _____ million Greebes. Other things constant, if the price of Greebes increased to $0.40 per Greebe, buyers would be willing to buy _____ million Greebes. Such a change would be a decrease in *(demand / quantity demanded)*. Other things constant, if the price of Greebes decreased to $0.20, buyers would be willing to buy _____ million Greebes. Such a change would be called an increase in *(demand / quantity demanded)*.

Adapted from Phillip Saunders, *Introduction to Microeconomics: Student Workbook,* 18th ed. (Bloomington, Ind., 1998). Copyright ©1998 Phillip Saunders. All rights reserved.

2. Now, let's suppose there is a dramatic change in federal income-tax rates that affects the disposable income of Greebe buyers. This change in the *ceteris paribus* (all else being equal) conditions underlying the original demand for Greebes will result in a new set of data, shown in Figure 3.3. Study these new data, and add the new demand curve for Greebes to the axes in Figure 3.2. Label the new demand curve D_1 and answer the questions that follow.

 Figure 3.3
New Demand for Greebes

Price ($ per Greebe)	Quantity Demanded (millions of Greebes)
$.05	300
.10	250
.15	200
.20	150
.25	100
.30	50

3. Comparing the new demand curve (D_1) with the original demand curve (D), we can say that the change in the demand for Greebes results in a shift of the demand curve to the *(left / right)*.

Such a shift indicates that at each of the possible prices shown, buyers are now willing to buy a *(smaller / larger)* quantity; and at each of the possible quantities shown, buyers are willing to offer a *(higher / lower)* maximum price. The cause of this demand curve shift was a(n) *(increase / decrease)* in tax rates that *(increased / decreased)* the disposable income of Greebe buyers.

4. Now, let's suppose that there is a dramatic change in people's tastes and preferences for Greebes. This change in the *ceteris paribus* conditions underlying the original demand for Greebes will result in a new set of data, shown in Figure 3.4. Study these new data, and add the new demand curve for Greebes to the axes in Figure 3.2. Label the new demand curve D_2 and answer the questions that follow.

 Figure 3.4
New Demand for Greebes

Price ($ per Greebe)	Quantity Demanded (millions of Greebes)
$.20	350
.25	300
.30	250
.35	200
.40	150
.45	100
.50	50

Comparing the new demand curve (D_2) with the original demand curve (D), we can say that the change in the demand for Greebes results in a shift of the demand curve to the *(left / right)*.

Advanced Placement Economics Macroeconomics: Student Activities © Council For Economic Education, New York, N.Y.

Such a shift indicates that at each of the possible prices shown, buyers are now willing to buy a *(smaller / larger)* quantity; and at each of the possible quantities shown, buyers are willing to offer a *(lower / higher)* maximum price. The cause of this shift in the demand curve was a(n) *(increase / decrease)* in people's tastes and preferences for Greebes.

Part B

Now, to test your understanding, underline the answer you think is the one best alternative in each of the following multiple-choice questions.

5. Other things constant, which of the following would *not* cause a change in the demand (shift in the demand curve) for mopeds?

   (A) A decrease in consumer incomes

   (B) A decrease in the price of mopeds

   (C) An increase in the price of bicycles, a substitute for mopeds

   (D) An increase in people's tastes and preferences for mopeds

6. "Rising oil prices have caused a sharp decrease in the demand for oil." Speaking precisely, and using terms as they are defined by economists, choose the statement that best describes this quotation.

   (A) The quotation is correct: An increase in price always causes a decrease in *demand*.

   (B) The quotation is incorrect: An increase in price always causes an increase in *demand*, not a decrease in *demand*.

   (C) The quotation is incorrect: An increase in price causes a decrease in the *quantity demanded*, not a decrease in *demand*.

   (D) The quotation is incorrect: An increase in price causes an increase in the *quantity demanded*, not a decrease in *demand*.

7. "As the price of domestic automobiles has inched upward, customers have found foreign autos to be a better bargain. Consequently, domestic auto sales have been decreasing, and foreign auto sales have been increasing." Using only the information in this quotation and assuming everything else constant, which of the following best describes this statement?

   (A) A shift in the demand curves for both domestic and foreign automobiles

   (B) A movement along the demand curves for both foreign and domestic automobiles

   (C) A movement along the demand curve for domestic autos, and a shift in the demand curve for foreign autos

   (D) A shift in the demand curve for domestic autos, and a movement along the demand curve for foreign autos

8. You hear a fellow student say: "Economic markets are like a perpetual see-saw. If demand rises, the price rises; if price rises, then demand will fall. If demand falls, price will fall; if price falls, demand will rise and so on forever." Dispel your friend's obvious confusion in no more than one short paragraph below.

Reasons for Changes in Demand

Part A

Read the eight newspaper headlines in Figure 4.2, and use the table to record the impact, if any, of each event on the demand for beef. Use the first column to the right of the headline to show whether the event causes a change in demand. Use the next column to record whether the change is an increase or a decrease in demand. In the third column, decide whether the demand curve shifts left or right. Finally, write the letter for the new demand curve. Use Figure 4.1 to help you. **Always start at curve B**, and move only one curve at a time. One headline implies that the demand for beef does not change.

 Figure 4.1
Beef Consumption in May

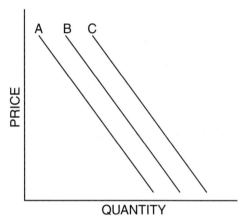

 Figure 4.2

Headline	Demand Shift? (Y / N)	If Demand Shifts, Inc / Dec	Curve Shifts Left / Right	New Curve
1. Price of Beef to Rise in June				
2. Millions of Immigrants Swell U.S. Population				
3. Pork Prices Drop				
4. Surgeon General Warns That Eating Beef Is Hazardous to Health				
5. Beef Prices Fall; Consumers Buy More				
6. Real Income for U.S. Drops for Third Month				
7. Charcoal Shortage Threatens Memorial Day Cookouts				
8. Nationwide Fad: The Disco-Burger				

Based on an activity from *Master Curriculum Guide in Economics: Teaching Strategies for High School Economics Courses* (New York: National Council on Economic Education, 1985), p. 68.

Part B

Categorize each change in demand in Part A according to the reason why demand changed. A given demand curve assumes that consumer expectations, consumer tastes and preferences, the number of consumers in the market, the income of consumers, and the prices of substitutes and complements are unchanged. In the table below, place an X next to the reason that the event described in the headline caused a change in demand. One headline will have no answer because it is a change in quantity demanded.

 Figure 4.3

↓ Reason Headline Number →	1	2	3	4	5	6	7	8
A change in consumer expectations								
A change in consumer tastes								
A change in the number of consumers in the market								
A change in income								
A change in the price of a substitute good								
A change in the price of a complementary good								

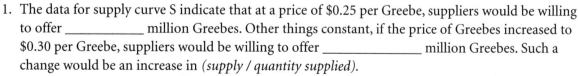
Supply Curves, Movements Along Supply Curves and Shifts in Supply Curves

In this activity and those that follow, we will assume that the long-run supply curve of Greebes is typically upward sloping.

Part A

Study the data in Figure 5.1 and plot the supply of Greebes on the axes in Figure 5.2. Label the supply curve S and answer the questions that follow. Write the correct answer on the answer blank, or underline the correct answer in parentheses.

 Figure 5.1
Supply of Greebes

Price ($ per Greebe)	Quantity Supplied (millions of Greebes)
$.15	100
.20	150
.25	200
.30	250
.35	300

 Figure 5.2
Supply of Greebes

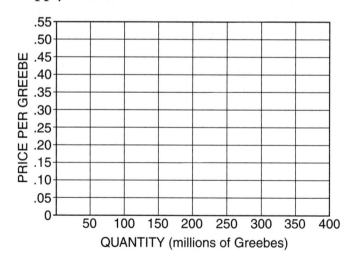

1. The data for supply curve S indicate that at a price of $0.25 per Greebe, suppliers would be willing to offer _____ million Greebes. Other things constant, if the price of Greebes increased to $0.30 per Greebe, suppliers would be willing to offer _____ million Greebes. Such a change would be an increase in *(supply / quantity supplied)*.

Adapted from Phillip Saunders, *Introduction to Microeconomics: Student Workbook,* 18th ed. (Bloomington, Ind., 1998).
Copyright © 1998 Phillip Saunders. All rights reserved. Modifications made by Helen Roberts, University of Illinois, Chicago, Ill.

Other things constant, if the price of Greebes decreased to $0.20 per Greebe, suppliers would be willing to offer _____ million Greebes. Such a change would be called a decrease in *(supply / quantity supplied)*.

2. Now, let's suppose that there is a dramatic change in the price of several of the raw materials used in making Greebes. This change in the *ceteris paribus* conditions underlying the original supply of Greebes will result in a new set of data, such as that shown in Figure 5.3. Study the data, and plot this supply of Greebes on the axes in Figure 5.2. Label the new supply curve S₁ and answer the questions that follow.

Figure 5.3
New Supply of Greebes

Price ($ per Greebe)	Quantity Supplied (millions of Greebes)
$.20	50
.25	100
.30	150
.35	200
.40	250

3. Comparing the new supply curve (S₁) with the original supply curve (S), we can say that a change in the supply of Greebes results in a shift of the supply curve to the *(left / right)*. Such a shift indicates that at each of the possible prices shown, suppliers are now willing to offer a *(smaller / larger)* quantity; and at each of the possible quantities shown, suppliers are willing to accept a *(higher / lower)* minimum price. The cause of this supply curve shift was a(n) *(increase / decrease)* in prices of several of the raw materials used in making Greebes.

4. Now, let's suppose that there is a dramatic change in the price of Silopanna, a resource used in the production of Greebes. This change in the *ceteris paribus* conditions underlying the original supply of Greebes will result in a new set of data shown in Figure 5.4. Study the data, and plot this supply of Greebes on the axes in Figure 5.2. Label the new supply curve S₂ and answer the questions that follow.

Figure 5.4
New Supply of Greebes

Price ($ per Greebe)	Quantity Supplied (millions of Greebes)
$.10	150
.15	200
.20	250
.25	300
.30	350

Comparing the new supply curve (S₂) with the original supply curve (S), we can say that the change in the supply of Greebes results in a shift of the supply curve to the *(left / right)*. Such a shift indicates that at each of the possible prices shown, suppliers are now willing to offer a *(smaller / larger)* quantity; and at each of the possible quantities shown, suppliers are willing to accept a *(lower / higher)* minimum price. The cause of this supply curve shift is a(n) *(increase / decrease)* in the price of Silopanna, a resource used in the production of Greebes.

Part B

Now, to check your understanding, underline the answer you think is the one best alternative in each of the following multiple-choice questions.

5. Other things constant, which of the following would *not* cause a change in the long-run supply of beef?
   (A) A decrease in the price of beef
   (B) A decrease in the price of cattle feed
   (C) An increase in the price of cattle feed
   (D) An increase in the cost of transporting cattle to market

6. "Falling oil prices have caused a sharp decrease in the supply of oil." Speaking precisely, and using terms as they are defined by economists, choose the statement that best describes this quotation.
   (A) The quotation is correct: A decrease in price always causes a decrease in *supply*.
   (B) The quotation is incorrect: A decrease in price always causes an increase in *supply*, not a decrease in *supply*.
   (C) The quotation is incorrect: A decrease in price causes an increase in the *quantity supplied*, not a decrease in *supply*.
   (D) The quotation is incorrect: A decrease in price causes a decrease in the *quantity supplied*, not a decrease in *supply*.

7. A multiyear drought in Florida has dried the land so that rampant wildfires have destroyed many orange groves. Florida oranges supply much of the nation's orange juice. Which statement below is correct?
   (A) The price of orange juice will rise because of a movement up the supply curve.
   (B) The price of orange juice will rise because the supply curve will shift to the left.
   (C) The price of orange juice will fall because of a movement down the supply curve.
   (D) The price of orange juice will fall because the supply curve will shift to the right.

8. A popular movie star wears a certain style of sunglasses. If her fans want to copy her look,
   (A) the price of the movie star's brand of sunglasses will rise because of a movement up the supply curve.
   (B) the price of the movie star's brand of sunglasses will rise because the supply curve will shift to the left.
   (C) the price of the movie star's brand of sunglasses will fall because of a movement down the supply curve.
   (D) the price of the movie star's brand of sunglasses will fall because the supply curve will shift to the right.

Reasons for Changes in Supply

Part A

Read the eight newspaper headlines in Figure 6.2, and record the impact, if any, of each event on the supply of cars. Use the first column to the right of the headline to show whether the event will cause a change in supply. Use the next column to record whether the change is an increase or a decrease in supply. In the third column, decide whether the supply curve shifts left or right. Finally, write the letter for the new supply curve. Use Figure 6.1 to help you. **Always start at curve B,** and move only one curve at a time. Two headlines imply that the supply of cars does not change.

 Figure 6.1

Supply of Foreign and Domestic Cars

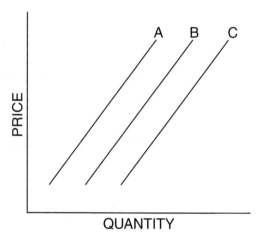

 Figure 6.2

Headline	Supply Shift? (Y / N)	If Supply Shifts, Inc / Dec	Curve Shifts Left / Right	New Curve
1. Auto Workers' Union Agrees to Wage Cuts				
2. New Robot Technology Increases Efficiency				
3. Nationwide Auto Strike Began at Midnight				
4. New Import Quotas Reduce Foreign Car Imports				
5. Cost of Steel Rises				
6. Auto Producer Goes Bankrupt; Closes Operation				
7. Buyers Reject New Models				
8. National Income Rises 2%				

From *Master Curriculum Guide in Economics: Teaching Strategies for High School Economics Courses* (New York: National Council on Economic Education, 1985), p. 69

Part B

Categorize each change in supply in Part A according to the reason why supply changed. In Figure 6.3, place an X next to the reason that the event described in the headline caused a change in supply. In some cases, more than one headline could be matched to a reason. Two headlines do not indicate a shift in supply.

 Figure 6.3

↓ Reason Headline Number →	1	2	3	4	5	6	7	8
A change in costs of inputs to production process								
A change in technology								
A change in the number of producers in the market								
Government policies								

Equilibrium Price and Equilibrium Quantity

Part A

Figure 7.1 below shows the demand for Greebes and the supply of Greebes. Plot these data on the axes in Figure 7.2. Label the demand curve D and label the supply curve S. Then answer the questions that follow. Fill in the answer blanks, or underline the correct answer in parentheses.

 Figure 7.1

Demand for and Supply of Greebes

Price ($ per Greebe)	Quantity Demanded (millions of Greebes)	Quantity Supplied (millions of Greebes)
$.15	300	100
.20	250	150
.25	200	200
.30	150	250
.35	100	300

 Figure 7.2

Demand for and Supply of Greebes

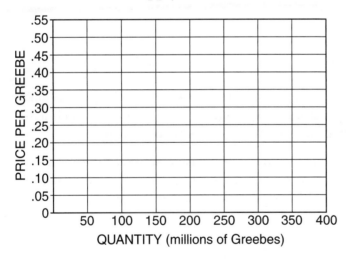

1. Under these conditions, competitive market forces would tend to establish an equilibrium price of _____ per Greebe and an equilibrium quantity of _____ million Greebes.

2. If the price currently prevailing in the market is $0.30 per Greebe, buyers would want to buy _____ million Greebes and sellers would want to sell _____ million Greebes. Under these conditions, there would be a (*shortage / surplus*) of _____ million Greebes. Competitive market forces would tend to cause the price to (*increase / decrease*) to a price of _____ per Greebe.

   At this new price, buyers would now want to buy _____ million Greebes, and sellers now want to sell _____ million Greebes. Because of this change in (*price / underlying conditions*),

Adapted from Phillip Saunders, *Introduction to Microeconomics: Student Workbook,* 18th ed. (Bloomington, Ind., 1998).

the (*demand / quantity demanded*) changed by _____ million Greebes, and the (*supply / quantity supplied*) changed by _____ million Greebes.

3. If the price currently prevailing in the market is $0.20 per Greebe, buyers would want to buy _____ million Greebes, and sellers would want to sell _____ million Greebes. Under these conditions, there would be a (*shortage / surplus*) of _____ million Greebes. Competitive market forces would tend to cause the price to (*increase / decrease*) to a price of _____ per Greebe. At this new price, buyers would now want to buy _____ million Greebes, and sellers now want to sell _____ million Greebes. Because of this change in (*price / underlying conditions*), the (*demand / quantity demanded*) changed by _____ million Greebes, and the (*supply / quantity supplied*) changed by _____ million Greebes.

4. Now, suppose a mysterious blight causes the supply schedule for Greebes to change to the following:

Figure 7.3
New Supply of Greebes

Price ($ per Greebe)	Quantity Supplied (millions of Greebes)
$.20	50
.25	100
.30	150
.35	200

Plot the new supply schedule on the axes in Figure 7.2 and label it S_1. Label the new equilibrium E_1. Under these conditions, competitive market forces would tend to establish an equilibrium price of _____ per Greebe and an equilibrium quantity of _____ million Greebes.

Compared with the equilibrium price in Question 1, we say that because of this change in (*price / underlying conditions*), the (*supply / quantity supplied*) changed; and both the equilibrium price and the equilibrium quantity changed. The equilibrium price (*increased / decreased*), and the equilibrium quantity (*increased / decreased*).

5. Now, with the supply schedule at S_1, suppose further that a sharp drop in people's incomes as the result of a prolonged recession causes the demand schedule to change to the following:

Figure 7.4
New Demand for Greebes

Price ($ per Greebe)	Quantity Demanded (millions of Greebes)
$.15	200
.20	150
.25	100
.30	50

Advanced Placement Economics Macroeconomics: Student Activities © Council For Economic Education, New York, N.Y.

Plot the new demand schedule on the axes in Figure 7.2 and label it D_1. Label the new equilibrium E_2. Under these conditions, with the supply schedule at S_1, competitive market forces would tend to establish an equilibrium price of _____ per Greebe and an equilibrium quantity of _____ million Greebes. Compared with the equilibrium price in Question 4, because of this change in *(price / underlying conditions)*, the *(demand / quantity demanded)* changed. The equilibrium price *(increased / decreased)*, and the equilibrium quantity *(increased / decreased)*.

6. The movement from the first equilibrium price and quantity to the new equilibrium price and quantity is the result of a *(price / nonprice)* effect.

Part B

The following questions refer to a group of related markets in the United States during a given time period. Assume that the markets are perfectly competitive and that the supply and demand model is completely applicable. The figures show the supply and demand in each market *before* the assumed change occurs. Trace through the effects of the assumed change, *other things constant*. Work your way from left to right. Shift only one curve in each market. For each market, draw whatever new supply or demand curves are needed, labeling each new curve S_1 or D_1. Then circle the correct symbol under each diagram (↑ for increase, — for unchanged, and ↓ for decrease). Remember to shift only one curve in each market.

7. Assume that a new fertilizer dramatically increases the amount of wheat that can be harvested with no additional labor or machinery. Also assume that this fertilizer does not affect potato farming and that people are satisfied to eat either bread made from wheat flour or potatoes.

 Figure 7.5
Effects of a New Fertilizer

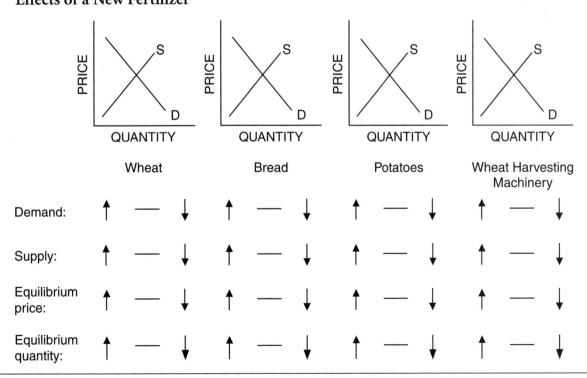

8. Assume that a heavy frost destroys half the world's coffee crop and that people use more cream in coffee than they do in tea.

 Figure 7.6
Effects of a Loss of Coffee Crop

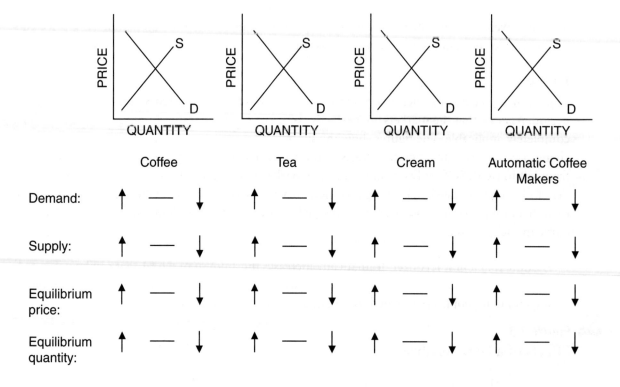

9. Assume beef and pork are perfect substitutes. The price of pork rises dramatically. Catsup is a complement to beef; mustard is a complement to pork.

 Figure 7.7

Effects of a Change in the Price of Pork

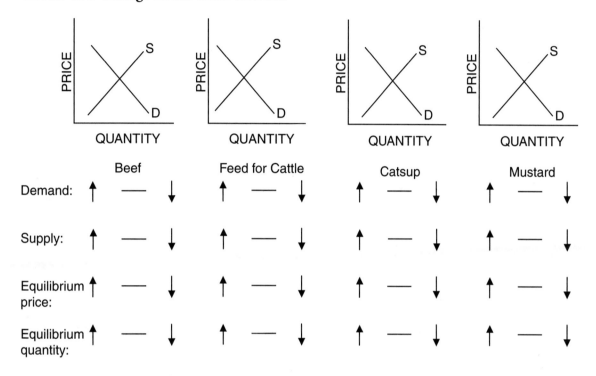

Elasticity: An Introduction

In many circumstances, it is not enough for an economist, policymaker, firm or consumer to simply know the direction in which a variable will be moving. For example, if I am a producer, the law of demand tells me that if I increase the price of my good, the quantity demanded by consumers will decrease. The law of demand doesn't tell me what will happen to my total revenue (the price of the good times the number of units sold), however. Whether total revenue increases or decreases depends on how responsive the quantity demanded is to the price change. Will it decrease a little? A lot? Throughout the discipline of economics, in fact, the responsiveness of one variable to changes in another variable is an important piece of information. In general, *elasticity* is a measurement of how responsive one variable is to a change in another variable — that is, how elastic one variable is given a change in the other, *ceteris paribus* (that is, holding all other variables constant).

Because elasticity measures responsiveness, changes in the variables are measured relative to some base or starting point. Consider the following elasticity measurements:

The price elasticity of demand, ε_d:

$$\varepsilon_d = \frac{percentage\ change\ in\ quantity\ demanded}{percentage\ change\ in\ price}$$

The income elasticity of demand, ε_d:

$$\varepsilon_d = \frac{percentage\ change\ in\ quantity\ demanded}{percentage\ change\ in\ income}$$

The price elasticity of supply, ε_s:

$$\varepsilon_s = \frac{percentage\ change\ in\ quantity\ supplied}{percentage\ change\ in\ price}$$

The wage elasticity of labor supply, ε_{ls}:

$$\varepsilon_{ls} = \frac{percentage\ change\ in\ quantity\ of\ labor\ supplied}{percentage\ change\ in\ wage}$$

Activity written by Kelly A. Chaston, Davidson College, Davidson, N.C.

Part A
Problems Involving Extra Credit

1. Now, suppose that your economics teacher currently allows you to earn extra credit by submitting answers to the end-of-the-chapter questions in your textbook. The number of questions you're willing to submit depends on the amount of extra credit for each question. How responsive you are to a change in the extra-credit points the teacher gives can be represented as an *elasticity*. Write the formula for the elasticity of extra-credit problems submitted:

$$\varepsilon_{ps} = \underline{\hspace{6cm}}$$

2. Now, consider that your teacher's goal is to get you to submit twice as many questions: a 100-percent increase. Underline the correct answer in parentheses.

   (A) If the number of chapter-end questions you submit *is* very responsive to a change in extra-credit points, then a given increase in extra credit elicits a large increase in questions submitted. In this case, your teacher will need to increase the extra-credit points by (*more than* / *less than* / *exactly*) 100 percent.

   (B) If the number of chapter-end questions you submit *is not* very responsive to a change in extra-credit points, then a given increase in extra credit elicits a small increase in questions submitted. In this case, your teacher will need to increase the extra-credit points by (*more than* / *less than* / *exactly*) 100 percent.

Advanced Placement Economics Macroeconomics: Student Activities © Council For Economic Education, New York, N.Y.

Part B
The Price Elasticity of Demand

It's easy to imagine that there are many applications for the elasticity concept. Here we will concentrate on the price elasticity of demand for goods and services. For convenience, the measure is repeated here:

$$\varepsilon_d = \frac{percentage\ change\ in\ quantity\ demanded}{percentage\ change\ in\ price}$$

Note the following points:

- Price elasticity of demand is always measured *along* a demand curve. When measuring the responsiveness of quantity demanded to a change in price, all other variables must be held constant.

- The price elasticity of demand is typically reported as a positive number, even though the calculation itself is negative; price and quantity demanded move in opposite directions.

- Along a linear demand curve, there are price ranges over which demand is elastic, unit elastic and inelastic.

 Figure 8.1

Relationship Between Changes in Quantity Demanded and Price

Percentage change in quantity demanded > percentage change in price	> 1	Elastic
Percentage change in quantity demanded = percentage change in price	= 1	Unit elastic
Percentage change in quantity demanded < percentage change in price	< 1	Inelastic

Part C
Calculating the Arc Elasticity Coefficient

The arc elasticity calculation method is obtained when the midpoint or average price and quantity are used in the calculation. This is reflected in the formula below.

$$\varepsilon_d = \frac{\text{percentage change in quantity demanded}}{\text{percentage change in price}} = \frac{\dfrac{Q - Q_1}{(Q + Q_1)/2}}{\dfrac{P - P_1}{(P + P_1)/2}} = \frac{\dfrac{\Delta Q}{(Q + Q_1)/2}}{\dfrac{\Delta P}{(P + P_1)/2}}$$

If we have the consumer or market demand curves, we can precisely calculate the arc elasticity value, or coefficient. Suppose that price is increased (decreased) from P to P_1 and so quantity demanded decreases (increases) from Q to Q_1.

Figure 8.2
Calculating the Arc Elasticity Coefficient

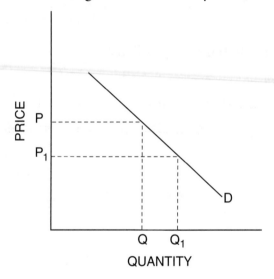

By making all numbers positive, we've in effect taken the absolute values of these changes, and so the elasticity coefficient will be positive. Note that we have used the average of the two prices and the two quantities. We have done this so that the elasticity measured will be the same whether we are moving from Q to Q_1 or the other way around.

Part D
Problems Involving Coffee

Suppose Moonbucks, a national coffee-house franchise, finally moves into the little town of Middle-ofnowhere. Moonbucks is the only supplier of coffee in town and faces the following demand schedule each week. Write the correct answer on the answer blanks, or underline the correct answer in parentheses.

 Figure 8.3

Cups of Coffee Demanded per Week

Price (per cup)	Quantity Demanded
$6	80
5	100
4	120
3	140
2	160
1	180
0	200

3. What is the arc price elasticity of demand when the price changes from $1 to $2? _____

$$\varepsilon_d = \frac{\dfrac{\Delta Q}{(Q + Q_1)/2}}{\dfrac{\Delta P}{(P + P_1)/2}} = \frac{\rule{2cm}{0.4pt}}{\rule{2cm}{0.4pt}} = \rule{2.5cm}{0.4pt}$$

So, over this range of prices, demand is (*elastic / unit elastic / inelastic*).

4. What is the arc price elasticity of demand when the price changes from $5 to $6? _____

$$\varepsilon_d = \frac{\dfrac{\Delta Q}{(Q + Q_1)/2}}{\dfrac{\Delta P}{(P + P_1)/2}} = \frac{\rule{2cm}{0.4pt}}{\rule{2cm}{0.4pt}} = \rule{2.5cm}{0.4pt}$$

So, over this range of prices, demand is (*elastic / unit elastic / inelastic*).

Note: Because the relationship between quantity demanded and price is inverse, price elasticity of demand would always be negative. Economists believe using negative numbers is confusing when referring to "large" or "small" elasticities of demand. Therefore, they use absolute or positive numbers, changing the sign on the negative numbers.

Part E

Now, consider Figure 8.4, which graphs the demand schedule given in Figure 8.3.

Recall the slope of a line is measured by the rise over the run: slope = rise / run = ΔP / ΔQ.

 Figure 8.4
Elasticity of Demand for Coffee

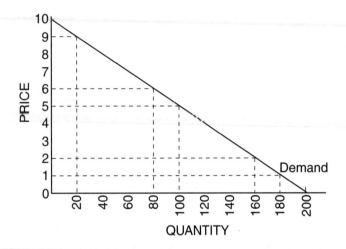

5. Using your calculations of ΔP and ΔQ from Question 3, calculate the slope of the demand curve.

   _____

6. Using your calculations of ΔP and ΔQ from Question 4, calculate the slope of the demand curve.

   _____

7. The law of demand tells us that an increase in price results in a decrease in the quantity demanded. Questions 5 and 6 remind us that the slope of a straight line is *constant everywhere along the
   line*. Along this demand curve, a change in price of $1 generates a change in quantity demanded of
   20 cups of coffee a week.

   You've now shown mathematically that while the slope of the demand curve is related to elasticity, the two concepts are not the same thing. Briefly discuss the relationship between where you
   are along the demand curve and the elasticity of demand. How does this tie into the notion of
   responsiveness?

Sample Multiple-Choice Questions

Circle the letter of each correct answer.

1. The crucial problem of economics is

    (A) establishing a fair tax system.

    (B) providing social goods and services.

    (C) developing a price mechanism that reflects the relative scarcities of products and resources.

    (D) allocating scarce productive resources to satisfy wants.

    (E) enacting a set of laws that protects resources from overuse.

2. When one decision is made, the next best alternative not selected is called

    (A) economic resource.

    (B) opportunity cost.

    (C) scarcity.

    (D) comparative disadvantage.

    (E) production.

3. Which of the following is true if the production possibilities curve is a curved line concave to the origin?

    (A) Resources are perfectly substitutable between the production of the two goods.

    (B) It is possible to produce more of both products.

    (C) Both products are equally capable of satisfying consumer wants.

    (D) The prices of the two products are the same.

    (E) As more of one good is produced, more and more of the other good must be given up.

4. Which of the following is true of the concept of increasing opportunity cost?

    (A) It is unimportant in command economies because of central planning.

    (B) It suggests that the use of resources to produce a set of goods and services means that as more of one is produced, some of the other must be sacrificed.

    (C) It is irrelevant if the production possibilities curve is convex to the origin.

    (D) It suggests that unlimited wants can be fulfilled.

    (E) It means that resources are plentiful and opportunities to produce greater amounts of goods and services are unlimited.

5. To be considered scarce, an economic resource must be which of the following?
    I.   Limited
    II. Free
    III. Desirable

    (A) I only

    (B) I and II only

    (C) II and III only

    (D) I and III only

    (E) I, II and III

6. The basic economic problem is reflected in which of the following concepts?
    I.   Opportunity cost
    II. Production possibilities
    III. The fallacy of composition
    IV. *Ceteris paribus*

    (A) I only

    (B) IV only

    (C) I and II only

    (D) II and III only

    (E) II, III and IV only

7. Which of the following goods would be considered scarce?

   I.   Education
   II. Gold
   III. Time

   (A) I only

   (B) II only

   (C) III only

   (D) I and II only

   (E) I, II and III

8. The value of the best alternative forgone when a decision is made defines

   (A) economic good.

   (B) opportunity cost.

   (C) scarcity.

   (D) trade-off.

   (E) comparative advantage.

9. Which of the following problems do all economic systems face?

   I.   How to allocate scarce resources among unlimited wants
   II. How to distribute income equally among all the citizens
   III. How to decentralize markets
   IV. How to decide what to produce, how to produce and for whom to produce

   (A) I only

   (B) I and IV only

   (C) II and III only

   (D) I, II and III only

   (E) I, II, III and IV

10. The opportunity cost of building a new high school is

    (A) the expense of hiring more teachers for the new high school.

    (B) the expense of new desks, chalkboards and books for the the new high school.

    (C) other goods and services, which must now be sacrificed to build the new high school.

    (D) overcrowded classrooms.

    (E) the bond levy needed to build the new high school.

11. In which way does a straight line production possibilities curve differ from a concave production possibilities curve?

    (A) A straight line production possibilities curve has a decreasing opportunity cost.

    (B) A straight line production possibilities curve has a constant opportunity cost.

    (C) A straight line production possibilities curve has an increasing opportunity cost.

    (D) A straight line production possibilities curve does not show opportunity cost.

    (E) There is no difference between the two production possibilities curves.

12. The law of increasing opportunity cost is reflected in the shape of the

    (A) production possibilities curve concave to the origin.

    (B) production possibilities curve convex to the origin.

    (C) horizontal production possibilities curve.

    (D) straight-line production possibilities curve.

    (E) upward-sloping production possibilities curve.

Use the figure below for questions 13 through 16. It shows the production possibilities curve for a country with full employment of a given-size labor force.

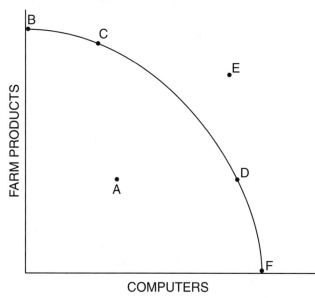

13. If the country is currently producing at Point C, it can produce more computers by doing which of the following?

   (A) Moving to Point A

   (B) Moving to Point B

   (C) Moving to Point D

   (D) Moving to Point E

   (E) Remaining at Point C, since computer production is maximized

14. Which of the following statements about the production possibilities curve is true?

   (A) Point A is not attainable in a developed society.

   (B) Point D is not attainable given the society's resources.

   (C) The relative position of Points C and D reflect production alternatives rather than relative prices.

   (D) Elimination of unemployment will move the production possibilities curve to the right, closer to Point E.

   (E) Point E lies outside the production possibilities curve because it represents a combination of resources not desired by the citizens of the country.

15. How might Point E be attained?

   (A) If the country's resources were more fully employed

   (B) If the country's resources were shifted to encourage more efficient use of scarce resources

   (C) If improvements in technology occurred in either the computer sector or the farm-products sector

   (D) If firms decreased their output of computers

   (E) If the nation used more of its scarce resources to produce farm products

16. Which of the following points would most likely lead to a rightward shift of the production possibilities curve over time?

   (A) Point A

   (B) Point B

   (C) Point C

   (D) Point D

   (E) Point E

17. The opportunity cost of producing an additional unit of product A is

   (A) all of the human and capital resources used to produce product A.

   (B) the retail price paid for product A.

   (C) the wholesale price of product A.

   (D) the amount of product B that cannot now be produced because of product A.

   (E) the profit that was earned from producing product A.

18. Which of the following would cause a leftward shift of the production possibilities curve?

   (A) An increase in unemployment

   (B) An increase in inflation

   (C) An increase in capital equipment

   (D) A decrease in consumer demand

   (E) A decrease in working-age population

19. Which of the following would cause an outward or rightward shift in the production possibilities curve?

   (A) An increase in unemployment

   (B) An increase in inflation

   (C) An increase in capital equipment

   (D) A decrease in natural resources

   (E) A decrease in the number of workers

Use the following table for questions 20, 21 and 22.

Mars		Venus	
Food	Clothing	Food	Clothing
0	30	0	40
2	24	4	32
4	18	8*	24*
5*	12*	12	16
8	6	16	8
10	0	20	0

Two nations, Mars and Venus, each produce food and clothing. The table above gives points on each nation's production possibilities curve. The asterisks indicate their current point of production.

20. In Mars, the opportunity cost of obtaining the first two units of food is how many units of clothing?

   (A) 2   (B) 3

   (C) 6   (D) 8

   (E) 12

21. In Venus, the opportunity cost of the first unit of

   (A) food is two units of clothing.

   (B) food is eight units of clothing.

   (C) clothing is two units of food.

   (D) clothing is four units of food.

   (E) clothing is eight units of food.

22. Which of the following statements is correct based on the concept of comparative advantage?

   (A) Mars and Venus should continue producing the quantities indicated by the asterisks.

   (B) Mars should specialize in the production of food.

   (C) Mars should specialize in the production of clothing.

   (D) Venus has the comparative advantage in clothing.

   (E) Mars has an absolute advantage in the production of food.

23. The table below shows the number of hours needed to produce one bushel of soybeans and one bushel of rice in each of two countries.

Country	One bushel of soybeans	One bushel of rice
U.S.	5 hours	7 hours
Japan	15 hours	10 hours

Which of the following statements must be true?

I. The United States has an absolute advantage in producing soybeans.

II. Japan has an absolute advantage in producing rice.

III. Japan has a comparative advantage in producing soybeans.

IV. The United States should specialize in the production of soybeans and Japan should specialize in the production of rice.

(A) I only

(B) III only

(C) I and IV only

(D) II and IV only

(E) I, II, III and IV

24. If there is an increase in demand for a good, what will most likely happen to the price and quantity of the good exchanged?

	Price	Quantity
(A)	Increase	Increase
(B)	Increase	Decrease
(C)	Decrease	Decrease
(D)	Decrease	Increase
(E)	No change	No change

25. If the demand for a good or service decreases, the equilibrium price and quantity are most likely to change in which of the following ways?

	Price	Quantity
(A)	Increase	Increase
(B)	Increase	Decrease
(C)	Decrease	Decrease
(D)	Decrease	Increase
(E)	No change	No change

26. A decrease in the price of silicon chips and increased production of user-friendly software will affect the price and quantity of computers in which of the following ways?

	Price	Quantity
(A)	Increase	Increase
(B)	Increase	Decrease
(C)	Decrease	Decrease
(D)	Decrease	May increase, decrease or remain the same
(E)	May increase, decrease or remain the same	Increase

27. An improvement in the technology used in the production of automobiles and an increase in the need for automobile transportation will most likely cause the price and quantity of automobiles to change in which of the following ways?

	Price	Quantity
(A)	Increase	Increase
(B)	Increase	Decrease
(C)	May increase, decrease, or stay the same	Increase
(D)	Decrease	May increase, decrease or remain the same
(E)	Decrease	Increase

28. An increase in the price of peanut butter will cause the demand curve for jelly to shift in which of the following directions?

    (A) To the right, because peanut butter is a product that the government says is good for you

    (B) To the right, if jelly is purchased by people with lower incomes and peanut butter is a luxury good for them

    (C) To the right, if peanut butter and jelly are complementary goods

    (D) To the left, if peanut butter and jelly are complementary goods

    (E) To the left, if peanut butter and jelly are substitute goods

29. According to the theory of comparative advantage, a good should be produced at the point where

    (A) its explicit costs are least.

    (B) its opportunity costs are least.

    (C) the cost of real resources used is least.

    (D) production can occur with the greatest increase in employment.

    (E) production can occur with the lowest increase in employment.

30. An increase in the price of gasoline will *most likely* cause the demand curve for tires to change in which direction?

    (A) To the left, because gasoline and tires are substitutes

    (B) To the left, because gasoline and tires are complements

    (C) To the right, because gasoline and tires are substitutes

    (D) To the right, because gasoline and tires are complements

    (E) To the right, because an increase in the price of gasoline makes consumers poorer and thus not willing to pay as much for tires

31. All of the following might reasonably be expected to shift the demand curve for beef to a new position *except*

    (A) a decrease in the price of beef.

    (B) a change in people's tastes with respect to beef.

    (C) an increase in the money incomes of beef consumers.

    (D) a widespread advertising campaign by the producers of a product competitive with beef, such as pork.

    (E) expectations that beef prices will fall in the future.

32. Specialization and trade will not take place in which of the following cases?

    I.   The opportunity costs of making two goods are the same in both countries.

    II. Wartime emergencies completely cut off trade routes.

    III. Tariff barriers increase the delivered cost of ordinary imported goods.

    (A) I only

    (B) II only

    (C) III only

    (D) I and II only

    (E) I, II and III

33. The Hatfields and McCoys have been fumin',
    fussin' and 'a fightin' for years. In the Hatfield
    family, a unit of cloth is worth 0.8 units of corn.
    At the McCoy's, a unit of cloth is worth 1.25
    units of corn. The Hatfields, however, produce
    more corn and cloth than the McCoys because
    they have higher quality resources. Despite the
    feud, is there a basis for specialization and trade?

    (A) No, the McCoys bring no net value to the
        community of Hatfield and McCoy.

    (B) No, the opportunity costs are the same for
        the Hatfields and the McCoys.

    (C) Yes, the Hatfields enjoy both a compara-
        tive and absolute advantage in cloth.

    (D) Yes, the Hatfields enjoy both a compara-
        tive and absolute advantage in corn.

    (E) Yes, the Hatfields enjoy both a compara-
        tive and absolute advantage in both corn
        and cloth.

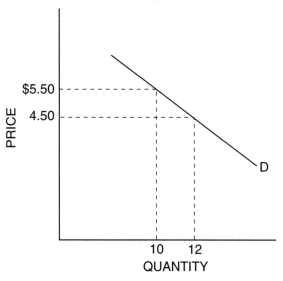

34. Between a price of $5.50 and $4.50, the demand
    curve in the figure above can be described as

    (A) perfectly elastic.

    (B) relatively elastic.

    (C) unit elastic.

    (D) relatively inelastic.

    (E) perfectly inelastic.

35. With a relatively elastic demand curve, if price
    increases by 10 percent, the quantity will most
    likely

    (A) increase by less than 10 percent.

    (B) increase by more than 10 percent.

    (C) decrease by less than 10 percent.

    (D) decrease by exactly 10 percent.

    (E) decrease by more than 10 percent.

36. "If you want to have anything done correctly,
    you have to do it yourself." This quote violates
    the principle of which of the following
    economic concepts?

    (A) Scarcity

    (B) Supply

    (C) Comparative advantage

    (D) Diminishing returns

    (E) Demand

Sample Short Free-Response Questions

1. True, false or uncertain, and explain why? "The economic concept of scarcity is not relevant to the study of a modern economy such as that of the United States because the existence of unsold stocks of goods (books, cars, homes) is vivid evidence that we are surrounded by plenty, not scarcity."

2. A newspaper headline says, "The Coldest Winter in 20 Years Brings Record Prices for Heating Oil."
    (A) Using a graph of home heating oil, show and explain how price changed.

    (B) What other factors could cause the price of heating oil to increase?

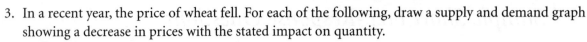
3. In a recent year, the price of wheat fell. For each of the following, draw a supply and demand graph showing a decrease in prices with the stated impact on quantity.

(A) The quantity of wheat decreasing

(B) The quantity of wheat increasing

(C) The quantity of wheat staying the same

4. True, false or uncertain, and explain why? "If you won $1 million in the lottery, you wouldn't have the economic problem of scarcity."

5. Explain what would have to be true in each case for the production possibilities curves to be shaped as they are in Graphs I, II and III.

Graph I

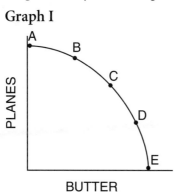

Graph II

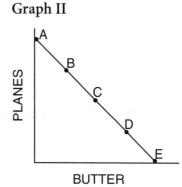

Graph III

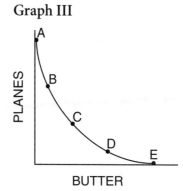

Sample Long Free-Response Questions

1. Every society has the fundamental problem of scarcity.

   (A) What is scarcity?

   (B) What three questions must every society answer because of scarcity?

   (C) What are the three ways societies have dealt with the scarcity problem?

   (D) Give one example of how each way is used in the United States.

2. Hightechland produces two commodities: movies and computers. Hightechland's resources include workers, factories, electricity and so on. The following schedule indicates some of the points on Hightechland's production possibilities curve.

Commodity	A	B	C	D	E
Movies	100	75	50	25	0
Computers	0	30	55	70	80

   (A) Does movie production exhibit increasing, decreasing or constant per-unit opportunity costs? How do you know?

   (B) Graph Hightechland's production possibilities curve, and label it AA.

(C) Suppose Hightechland is operating at Point C but would like to alter production to Point D. What would be the per-unit opportunity cost of producing more computers?

(D) Suppose Hightechland is operating at Point C but would like to alter production to Point B. What would be the per-unit opportunity cost of producing more movies?

(E) What will happen to Hightechland's production possibilities curve if many of its movie sets are destroyed by fire? (Assume that the sets are not used in the production of computers.) Using the same graph you drew for Question 2(B), draw Hightechland's new production possibilities curve and label it BB.

(F) What will happen to Hightechland's production possibilities curve if all the country's resources are reduced (perhaps by natural disaster or war)? Using the same graph as in Question 2(B), draw Hightechland's new production possibilities curve and label it CC.

(G) What will happen to Hightechland's production possibilities curve if technology improves both the production of movies and the production of computers? Using the same graph as in Question 2(B), draw Hightechland's new production possibilities curve and label it DD.

3. The market for many commodities is seasonal in nature. Their sales (equilibrium quantity) increase dramatically during certain times of the year. Christmas cards and fresh strawberries, at least in the North, are two examples. Christmas card sales increase during the last three months of the year, and the sales of fresh strawberries in the North increase during the summer months. But the (equilibrium) price movement of these two commodities is quite different during their peak sales season: Christmas cards increase in price during the last three months of the year, whereas strawberries decrease in price during the summer.

(A) Show on the graph below how there can be an increase in the equilibrium quantity and an increase in the equilibrium price of Christmas cards during the last three months of the year, and briefly explain what has happened.

Christmas Card Market

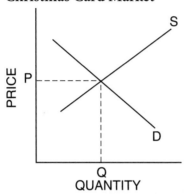

(B) Change the graph for fresh strawberries in the North to show how there can be an increase in the equilibrium quantity and a decrease in the equilibrium price of strawberries in the summer, and briefly explain what has happened.

Strawberry Market in the North

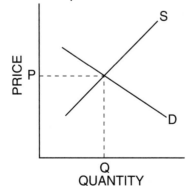

4. Explain how each of the following may affect the production possibilities curve of the United States or the point at which the economy is operating. Draw a production possibilities curve; put "Capital Goods" on the vertical axis and "Consumer Goods" on the horizontal axis. Now, add a PPC curve or point to the graph to illustrate the scenario.

(A) The Congress and the president decide to provide more funding for higher education with more students attending college and graduating.

(B) New advances in medicine allow for a healthier lifestyle.

(C) The United States agrees to be a part of a world-trade agreement that will foster international trade.

(D) The unemployment rate increases in the economy from 4.2 percent to 5.1 percent of the labor force.

(E) Computer viruses are out of control, and efficiency and output in the economy fall.

Macroeconomics | Unit 2

Measuring Economic Performance

■ Macroeconomics is the study of the economy as a whole; microeconomics is the study of individual parts of the economy such as businesses, households and prices. Macroeconomics looks at the forest; microeconomics looks at the trees.

■ A circular flow diagram illustrates the major flows of goods and services, resources and income in an economy. It shows how changes in these flows can alter the level of goods and services, employment and income.

■ Gross domestic product (GDP) is the market value of all final goods and services produced in a nation in one year. It is the most important measurement of production and output.

■ GDP counts only final goods and services; it does not count intermediate goods and services.

■ GDP also does not count secondhand goods; the buying and selling of stocks and bonds; and transfer payments such as Social Security benefits, unemployment compensation and certain interest payments.

■ GDP includes profits earned by foreign-owned businesses and income earned by foreigners in the United States, but it excludes profits earned by U.S.-owned companies overseas and income earned by U.S. citizens who work abroad.

■ GDP may be calculated in two ways:

1. Add all the consumption, investment and government expenditures plus net exports or

2. Add all the incomes received by owners of productive resources in the economy.

■ Price indexes measure price changes in the economy. They are used to compare the prices of a given bundle or market basket of goods and services in one year with the prices of the same bundle or market basket in another year.

■ A price index has a base year, and the price level in that year is given an index number of 100. The price level in all other years is expressed in relation to the price level in the base year.

$$\text{Price index number} = \frac{\text{weighted cost of base-period items in current-year prices}}{\text{weighted cost of base-period items in base-year prices}} \times 100$$

■ The most frequently used price indexes are the GDP price deflator, the consumer price index (CPI) and the producer price index (PPI).

■ Real GDP is adjusted for price changes; nominal GDP is not adjusted for price changes.

■ Inflation is a general increase in the overall price level.

■ Savers, lenders and people on fixed incomes generally are hurt by unanticipated inflation; borrowers gain from unanticipated inflation.

■ Unemployment occurs when people who are willing and able to work cannot find jobs at satisfactory wage rates.

■ Unemployment is classified into three categories: frictional, cyclical and structural.

■ The unemployment rate represents people who are not working but who are actively looking for a job.

■ Full employment is not defined as zero unemployment because frictional and structural unemployment exist even with zero cyclical unemployment.

■ The unemployment rate at full employment is called the natural rate of unemployment.

■ The labor force is defined as people who have a job (employed) and people who are actively looking for a job (unemployed). The labor force participation rate is the percentage of the population over the age of 16 that is in the labor force.

■ A business cycle describes the ups and downs of economic activity over a period of years.

■ The phases of the business cycle are expansion (recovery), peak, contraction (recession) and trough.

Test of Macroeconomic Thinking

Circle T for true or F for false in the statements that follow.

T   F   1. If a country could maintain a high economic growth rate, the country would eventually be able to satisfy everyone's wants for goods and services.

T   F   2. If all the nations of the world disarmed, the international economy would collapse into a long depression and unemployment would increase.

T   F   3. Money is an important economic resource.

T   F   4. The higher the GDP, the better off all the people of the country are.

T   F   5. Full employment means zero unemployment.

T   F   6. The United States has had an inflation rate of at least 3 percent for each of the last 50 years.

T   F   7. Unanticipated inflation hurts almost everyone.

T   F   8. Money consists mainly of currency and coins and is created by government printing presses and mints.

T   F   9. The value of the dollar is determined by the fact that it is backed by gold.

T   F   10. Most economists believe the only purpose of taxes is to provide money for government.

T   F   11. The chief task of the Federal Reserve System is to insure the deposits of bank customers.

T   F   12. Tariffs are needed to protect our standard of living from competition from cheap foreign labor.

Activity written by John Morton, National Council on Economic Education, New York, N.Y.

Understanding the Circular Flow of the Macroeconomy

Firms provide goods and services to households through the product markets. Households pay for these goods and services with money. Households supply firms with productive resources: labor, land, capital and entrepreneurial skills. Firms pay money income to households. The value of income firms pay to households, including the profits that business owners receive, equals the dollar value of output. Firms and households decide how much to buy or sell in the markets for goods and resources. For example, Tran spends $10.00 on school supplies at the market, buying goods and paying with money. The market owner uses the $10.00 to pay part of the salary of Mariko, the cashier. The firm is buying resources and paying for them with money. The $10.00 is now ready to be spent in another round. Firms and households pay taxes and user fees to the government, which provides them with some goods and services, such as police protection and national defense.

 Figure 10.1

The Circular Flow of Resources, Goods, Services and Money Payments

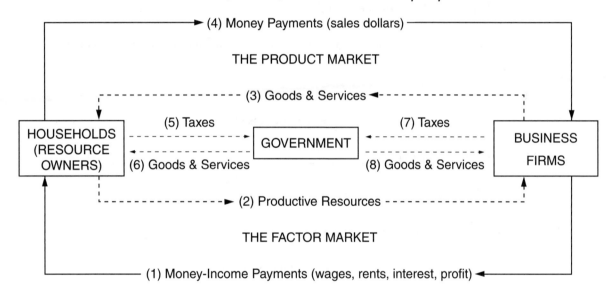

Activity written by Helen Roberts, University of Illinois, Chicago, Ill.

Part A

Each of the flows in the circular flow diagram in Figure 10.1 is numbered. Identify which number matches the transaction described in the statements below. Consider only the first transaction — not the return flow.

1. David buys a CD at the local store for $9.99. _____

2. Emily earns $6.50 per hour entering data at the music conservatory. _____

3. Maria pays her federal income tax. _____

4. Jagdish receives $15,000 in profits from his half-ownership of a coffee shop. _____

5. Keisha makes decorative pillows that she sells for $30.00. _____

6. Mammoth Toys Inc. hires 100 new employees. _____

7. The National Park Service opens two new campgrounds in Yellowstone National Park.

Part B

Write T if the statement is true and F if the statement is false.

8. Money flows are clockwise. _____

9. Goods and services flows are clockwise. _____

10. The resource market determines the price per acre of farmland. _____

11. The product market determines the price of a computer. _____

12. Firms sell resources in the resource markets. _____

13. Government buys resources and households sell resources. _____

14. Government buys products, and firms sell products. _____

15. The product market determines the salary of the C.E.O. of a firm. _____

16. The resource market determines the price of soda. _____

17. The resource market determines the price of soda-bottling equipment. _____

Measuring Broad Economic Goals

Overview

The 1930s were marked by periods of chronically high unemployment in the United States. After World War II, Congress passed the Employment Act of 1946, which stated that it was the policy and responsibility of the federal government to use all practical means to promote maximum employment, production and purchasing power. The Employment Act of 1946 established three important goals for the economy:

1. *Full employment* (also called the natural level of employment) exists when most individuals who are willing to work at the prevailing wages in the economy are employed and the average price level is stable. Even under conditions of full employment, there will be some temporary unemployment as workers change jobs and as new workers seek their first jobs (*frictional* unemployment). In addition, there will be some *structural* unemployment. Structural unemployment exists because there is a mismatch between the skills of the people seeking jobs and the skills required for available jobs.

2. *Price stability* exists when the average level of prices in the economy is neither increasing nor decreasing. The goal of price stability does not imply that prices of individual items should not change — only that the average level of prices should not. A sustained rise in the average level of prices is called *inflation*; a sustained decline is called *deflation*.

3. *Economic growth* exists when the economy produces increasing amounts of goods and services over the long term. If the increase is greater than the increase in population, the amount of goods and services available per person will rise, and thus the nation's standard of living will improve.

In 1978, Congress passed the Full Employment and Balanced Growth (Humphrey-Hawkins) Act establishing two additional goals: an unemployment rate of 4 percent with a zero-percent inflation rate.

Measuring the Achievement of Economic Goals

To determine how well we are achieving the economic goals, we must measure the levels of employment, prices and economic growth. We look at how such measurements are commonly made.

Part A
Measuring Employment

The civilian unemployment rate measures how well we are achieving the goal of full employment. The unemployment rate is derived from a national survey of about 60,000 households. Each month the federal government asks these households about the employment status of household members aged 16 and older (adult population). The survey puts each person in one of three categories: employed, unemployed or not in the labor force. People who are at work (the employed) plus those who are actively looking for work (the unemployed) make up the *labor force*. The labor force is much smaller than the total adult population because many individuals are too old to work, some people are unable to work and some choose not to work.

Adapted from *Master Curriculum Guide in Economics: Teaching Strategies for High School Economics Courses* (New York: National Council on Economic Education, 1985), p. 126.

The *unemployment rate* (UR) is defined as

$$UR = \frac{\text{number of unemployed}}{\text{labor force}} \times 100$$

The *labor force participation rate* (LFPR) is defined as:

$$LFPR = \frac{\text{number in labor force}}{\text{adult population}} \times 100$$

How well has the U.S. economy met the goal of full employment? Use the formulas just given to fill in the last three columns of Figure 11.1. All of the population and labor-force data are in millions.

Figure 11.1
Civilian Employment 1960 to 2000

Year	Civilian Noninstitutional Population Aged 16 and Over	Civilian Labor Force			Unemployment Rate	Labor Force Participation Rate
		Employed	Unemployed	Total		
1960	117	66	4			
1970	137	79	4			
1980	168	99	8			
1990	188	117	7			
2000	209	135	6			

1. In which year was the economy very close to full employment as indicated in the Humphrey-Hawkins Act?

2. Why has the labor force participation rate increased since the 1960s?

3. Do the data on the national unemployment rate in Figure 11.1 reflect the extent of unemployment among a particular group in our society, such as teenagers aged 16 to 19? Explain.

Part B
Measuring Price Changes

Price indexes measure price changes in the economy. By using a price index, you can combine the prices of a number of goods and/or services and express in one number the average change for all the prices. The consumer price index, or CPI, is the measure of price changes that is probably most familiar to people. It measures changes in the prices of goods and services commonly bought by consumers. Items on which the average consumer spends a great deal of money — such as food — are given more weight (importance) in computing the index than items such as newspapers, magazines and books, on which the average consumer spends comparatively less.

The index itself is based on a market basket of approximately 400 goods and services weighted according to how much the average consumer spent in the base year. Other price indexes used in the United States include

- the producer price index, which measures changes in the prices of consumer goods before they reach the retail level, as well as the prices of supplies and equipment businesses buy, and

- the gross domestic product price deflator, or GDP price deflator, which is the most inclusive index available because it takes into account all goods and services produced.

To construct any price index, economists select a previous period, usually one year, to serve as the base period. The prices of any subsequent period are expressed as a percentage of the base period. For convenience, the base period of almost all indexes is set at 100.

For the consumer price index, the formula used to measure price change from the base period is

$$\text{Consumer price index} = \frac{\text{weighted cost of base-period items in current-year prices}}{\text{weighted cost of base-period items in base-year prices}} \times 100$$

We multiply by 100 to express the index relative to the figure of 100 for the base period.

To keep things simple, let's say an average consumer in our economy buys only three items, as described in Figure 11.2. First compute the cost of buying all the items in the base year:

```
30  x  $5.00   =    $150
40  x  $6.00   =     240
60  x  $1.50   =      90
TOTAL          =    $480
```

To compute the consumer price index for Year 1 in Figure 11.2, find the cost of buying these same items in Year 1. Try this yourself. Your answer should be $530: the sum of (30 x $7) + (40 x $5) + (60 x $2). The consumer price index for Year 1 is then equal to ($530 / $480) x 100, which equals 110.4. This means that what we could have bought for $100 in the base year costs $110.40 in Year 1.

If we subtract the base year index of 100.0 from 110.4, we get the percentage change in prices from the base year. In this example, prices rose 10.4% from the base year to Year 1.

Remember that the weights used for the consumer price index are determined by what consumers bought in the base year; in the example we used base-year quantities to figure the expenditures in

Year 1 as well as in the base year. The rate of change in this index is determined by looking at the percentage change from one year to the next. If, for example, the consumer price index were 150 in one year and 165 the next, then the year-to-year percentage change is 10 percent. You can compute the change using this formula:

$$\text{Price change} = \frac{\text{change in CPI}}{\text{beginning CPI}} \times 100$$

Here's the calculation for the example above:

$$\text{Price change} = \frac{165 - 150}{150} \times 100 = 10\%$$

Fill in the blanks in Figure 11.2, and then use the data to answer the questions.

✳ Figure 11.2
Prices of Three Goods Compared with Base-Year Price

	Quantity Bought in Base Year	Unit Price in Base Year	Spending in Base Year	Unit Price in Year 1	Spending in Year 1	Unit Price in Year 2	Spending in Year 2
Whole pizza	30	$5.00	$150	$7.00	$210	$9.00	$270
Prerecorded audio cassette	40	6.00	$240	5.00	$200	4.00	$160
Six-pack of soda	60	1.50	$90	2.00	$120	2.50	$150
Total	—	—	$480	—	$530	—	$580

4. What is the total cost of buying all the items in Year 2? ___$580___

5. What is the CPI for Year 2? ___120.8___ $\frac{580}{480} \times 100 = 120.8$

6. What is the percentage increase in prices from the base year to Year 2? ___20.8%___

   120.8 − 100 = 20.8%
   CPI − 100 = % increase in prices

7. In August 2000 the CPI was 172.8, and in August 2001 the CPI was 177.50. What was the percentage change in prices for this 12-month period? ___2.72%___

   $\frac{177.5 - 172.8}{172.8} \times 100 = 2.72\%$

Part C
Measuring Short-Run Economic Growth

To measure fluctuations in output (short-run economic growth), we measure increases in the quantity of goods and services produced in the economy from quarter to quarter or year to year. The *gross domestic product*, or GDP, is commonly used to measure economic growth. The GDP is the dollar value at market prices of all final goods and services produced in the economy during a stated period.

Final goods are goods intended for the final user. For example, gasoline is a final good; but crude oil, from which gasoline and other products are derived, is not.

Before using GDP to measure output growth, we must first adjust GDP for price changes. Let's say GDP in Year 1 is $1,000 and in Year 2 it is $1,100. Does this mean the economy has grown 10 percent between Year 1 and Year 2? Not necessarily. If prices have risen, part of the increase in GDP in Year 2 will merely represent the increase in prices. We call GDP that has been adjusted for price changes *real* GDP. If it isn't adjusted for price changes, we call it *nominal* GDP.

To compute real GDP in a given year, use the following formula:

Real GDP in Year 1 = (nominal GDP x 100) / price index

To compute real output growth in GDP from one year to another, subtract real GDP for Year 2 from real GDP in Year 1. Divide the answer (the change in real GDP from the previous year) by real GDP in Year 1. The result, multiplied by 100, is the percentage growth in real GDP from Year 1 to Year 2. (If real GDP declines from Year 1 to Year 2, the answer will be a negative percentage.) Here's the formula:

$$\text{Output growth} = \frac{(\text{real GDP in Year 2} - \text{real GDP in Year 1})}{\text{real GDP in Year 1}} \times 100$$

For example, if real GDP in Year 1 = $1,000 and in Year 2 = $1,028, then the output growth rate from Year 1 to Year 2 is 2.8%: (1,028 − 1,000) / 1,000 = .028, which we multiply by 100 in order to express the result as a percentage.

To understand the impact of output changes, we usually look at real GDP per capita. To do so, we divide the real GDP of any period by a country's average population during the same period. This procedure enables us to determine how much of the output growth of a country simply went to supply the increase in population and how much of the growth represented improvements in the standard of living of the entire population. In our example, let's say the population in Year 1 was 100 and in Year 2 it was 110. What was real GDP per capita in Years 1 and 2?

Year 1

$$\text{Real GDP per capita} = \frac{\text{Year 1 real GDP}}{\text{population in Year 1}} = \frac{\$1,000}{100} = \$10$$

Year 2

$$\text{Real GDP per capita} = \frac{\$1,028}{110} = \$9.30$$

In this example, the average standard of living fell even though output growth was positive. Developing countries with positive output growth but high rates of population growth often experience this condition.

Now try these problems using the information in Figure 11.3.

 Figure 11.3
Nominal and Real GDP

	Nominal GDP	Price Index	Population
Year 3	$5,000	125	11
Year 4	$6,600	150	12

8. What is the real GDP in Year 3? ____4,000____

9. What is the real GDP in Year 4? ____4,400____

10. What is the real GDP per capita in Year 3? ___363.64___

11. What is the real GDP per capita in Year 4? ___366.67___

12. What is the rate of real output growth between Years 3 and 4? _____10%_____

13. What is the rate of real output growth per capita between Years 3 and 4? _____.83%_____
    (Hint: Use per-capita data in the output growth rate formula.)

$$\frac{5000 \times 100}{125} = \frac{500,000}{125} = 4,000$$

$$\frac{6600 \times 100}{150} = \frac{660,000}{150} =$$

$$\frac{4000}{11} =$$

$$\frac{366.67 - 363.64}{363.64} \times 100 =$$

$$\frac{4400 - 4000}{4000}$$

All About GDP

Part A
Is This Counted as Part of GDP?

Which of the following are *included* and which are *excluded* in calculating GDP? Explain your decisions.

1. A monthly check received by an economics student who has been granted a government scholarship

2. A farmer's purchase of a new tractor

3. A plumber's purchase of a two-year-old used truck

4. Cashing a U.S. government bond

5. The services of a mechanic in fixing the radiator on his own car

6. A Social Security check from the government to a retired store clerk

7. An increase in business inventories

8. The government's purchase of a new submarine for the Navy

9. A barber's income from cutting hair

10. Income received from the sale of Nike stock

Part A adapted from William B. Walstad, Michael W. Watts, Robert F. Smith and Campbell R. McConnell, *Instructor's Manual to Accompany Economics,* 10th ed. (New York: McGraw-Hill Book Co., 1987), p. 33. Parts B and C written by John Morton, National Council on Economic Education, New York, N.Y.

Part B
GDP: Is It Counted and Where?

For each of the following items, write one of the following in the space provided:

        C if the item is counted as *consumption spending.*
        I if the item is counted as *investment spending.*
        G if the item is counted as *government spending.*
        NX if the item is counted as *net exports.*
        NC if the item is *not counted* in GDP.

____ 11. You spend $7.00 to attend a movie.

____ 12. A family pays a contractor $100,000 for a house he built for them this year.

____ 13. A family pays $75,000 for a house built three years ago.

____ 14. An accountant pays a tailor $175 to sew a suit for her.

____ 15. The government increases its defense expenditures by $1,000,000,000.

____ 16. The government makes a $300 Social Security payment to a retired person.

____ 17. You buy General Motors Corp. stock for $1,000 in the stock market.

____ 18. At the end of a year, a flour-milling firm finds that its inventories of grain and flour are $10,000 above the amounts of its inventories at the beginning of the year.

____ 19. A homemaker works hard caring for her spouse and two children.

____ 20. Ford Motor Co. buys new auto-making robots.

____ 21. You pay $300 a month to rent an apartment.

____ 22. Apple Computer Co. builds a new factory in the United States.

____ 23. R.J. Reynolds Co. buys control of Nabisco.

____ 24. You buy a new Toyota that was made in Japan.

____ 25. You pay tuition to attend college.

Part C
Why Are Items Counted or Not Counted in GDP?

26. We count only the final retail price of a new good or service in GDP. Why?

27. A purely financial transaction will not be counted in GDP. Why?

28. When a homeowner does home-improvement work, the value of the labor is not counted in GDP. Why?

Price Indexes

There is more than one method for constructing a price index. The easiest to understand is probably the *weighted-average* method explained in this activity. This method compares the total cost of a fixed market basket of goods in different years. The total cost is weighted by multiplying the price of each item in the basket by the number of units of the item in the basket and then adding up all the prices. The cost of the basic market basket in the current year is then expressed as a percentage of the cost of the basic market basket in the base year using this formula:

$$\text{index number} = \frac{\text{current-year cost}}{\text{base-year cost}} \times 100$$

Multiplying by 100 converts the number so it is comparable to the base-year number. The base year always has an index number of 100 since the current-year cost and the base-year cost of the market basket are the same in the base year.

Part A
Constructing a Price Index

Using this information, let us now construct a price index. Fill in the blanks in Figure 13.1.

  Figure 13.1
Constructing a Price Index

Basic Market Basket Item	No. of Units	Year 1		Year 2 ✓		Year 3	
		Price Per Unit	Cost of Market Basket	Price Per Unit	Cost of Market Basket	Price Per Unit	Cost of Market Basket
Cheese	2 lbs.	$1.75	$3.50	$1.50	$3.00	$1.50	$3.00
Blue Jeans	2 pair	12.00	24.00	15.50	31.00	20.00	40.00
Gasoline	10 gals.	1.25	12.50	1.60	16.00	2.70	27.4
Total Expenditure	14	—	$40.00	—	$50.00	—	$70

BASE YEAR COST IS ALWAYS 100

1. We now have the information needed to construct a price index. The first step is to pick a base year and apply the formula. If Year 1 is selected as the base year, the index number for Year 1 is ($40 / $40) x 100 = 100. The index number for Year 2 is ($50 / $40) x 100 = 125 and the index number for Year 3 is (✓ $70 / $40) x 100 = 175 .

2. These index numbers indicate that there was a 25 percent increase in prices between Year 1 and Year 2.

  (A) What is the percentage increase between Year 1 and Year 3? 75% . $\frac{175-100}{100} = 75\%$

  (B) What is the percentage increase between Year 2 and Year 3? 40% . $\frac{175-125}{125} = \frac{50}{125} = .4 = 40\%$

YEAR 1 → YEAR 2
$\frac{Y2-Y1}{Y1} = \frac{125-100}{100}$
$= \frac{25}{100} = .25 = 25\%$

YOU CAN DO THIS W/ BOTH COST #S and INDEX #S.

Part B
Changing the Base Year

We need not have chosen Year 1 to be our base year. To determine if our choice of base year influenced the results, let's use Year 2 as our base year and recompute both the index numbers and the percentage changes between years. The first percentage change in prices has been done for you.

 Figure 13.2

Changing the Base Year of a Price Index

Year	Index Numbers (Year 2 = Base)	Percentage Change in Prices (calculated by using changes in index numbers)	
Year 1	($40 / $50) x 100 = 80	Between Yr. 1 and Yr. 2	([100 − 80] / 80) x 100 = 25%
Year 2	($50 / $50) x 100 = 100	Between Yr. 2 and Yr. 3	([140 − 100] / 100) x 100 = 40%
Year 3	($70 / $50) x 100 = 140	Between Yr. 1 and Yr. 3	([140 − 80] / 80) x 100 = 75%

3. Do the index numbers change when the base year is changed from Year 1 to Year 2? __yes__

4. Does the percentage change in prices between years change when the base year is changed from Year 1 to Year 2? __no__ Why or why not?
percentage growth in the prices have not changed at all.

5. Would the price index numbers you have computed above change if a different set of expenditure patterns were selected for weighting? _____ Why?

6. Under what conditions would each price index number computed above be a cost-of-living index?

7. Would each price index number computed above be accurate if the quality of the goods in the basic market basket changed? _____ Explain why.

8. How do you know if the quality of a product changes for the better? For the worse?

Advanced Placement Economics Macroeconomics: Student Activities © Council For Economic Education, New York, N.Y.

Inflation Game: Royalty for a Day

Introduction

Prices usually rise over a period of time. The same items you bought a few years ago may cost more now. For example, a restaurant menu lists its finest steak entrée at $22; however, two years ago the same steak was only $20. *Inflation* is the term used to describe an increase in the overall level of prices. It's an important concept to understand because it's discussed so frequently in the media: Price indexes and inflation measurements are reported almost daily in the financial pages, politicians constantly announce programs to control inflation and economists endlessly debate inflation's effects on economic growth.

In general, people don't like inflation because higher prices mean they can purchase less for the same income. However, inflation does not affect everyone in the same way. While many people are hurt by inflation, especially when it is unexpected, others may actually benefit.

This activity is designed to teach you the effects of inflation on different segments of the population: Who is hurt by unanticipated inflation and who benefits?

Overview of the Game

This activity is modeled after an ancient (1950s) television game show called "Queen for a Day," in which (women) contestants took turns describing their lives of tragedy, hardship and sorrow. After all had shared their misery, the sympathetic audience voted for the most deserving by applauding. An "applause meter" measured the sound. The winner was crowned "Queen for a Day" and presented with a robe, crown and many prizes. In this modern version, male and female economics students compete for the honor of "Royalty for a Day" by convincing the audience how much they are suffering because of inflation. Your teacher will provide additional information.

Part A
Audience Scorecard

Using the scorecard on the next page, indicate who is hurt or helped by inflation and give the reason why you think so.

Activity written by Joanne Benjamin, Los Gatos High School, Los Gatos, Calif.

Audience Scorecard

Contestant	Gain or Hurt by Inflation?	Reasoning
Priscilla *Homeowner / Worker*		
Mayor *Government official*		
Peter *Store owner*		
Theresa *Auto worker /* *Union member*		
Jerry *Real-estate developer /* *Speculator*		
Elmer *Retiree*		
Mr. Sad Class *Teacher*		
Lucy *High school senior*		
Bernie *Bank president*		
Helga *Retiree*		
Jerome *Potential homeowner /* *Borrower*		
Lawrence *British* *businessowner*		

Part B
Spectrum Technique for Analyzing Contestants
Distribute the contestants along the spectrum, and explain why you think each should be located where you put him or her.

 Figure 14.1
Spectrum Technique for Analyzing Contestants

Suffers most   Neutral   Benefits most
from inflation   (neither suffers nor benefits)   from inflation

Hello.

Hello.
Bitch.

Helb!
Kumusta

Who Is Hurt and Who Is Helped by Unanticipated Inflation?

In Questions 1 through 15 decide which people or groups are hurt by unanticipated inflation and which benefit from unanticipated inflation. Circle the correct response, and explain why you answered as you did.

> H means the person or group is *hurt* by unanticipated inflation.
>
> G means the person or group *gains* from unanticipated inflation.
>
> U means it is *uncertain* if the person or group is affected by unanticipated inflation or if the effects are unclear.

1. Banks extend many fixed-rate loans.

   (H)   G   U

   Explain:

2. A farmer buys machinery with a fixed-rate loan to be repaid over a 10-year period.

   H   (G)   U

   Explain:

3. Your family buys a new home with an adjustable-rate mortgage.

   H   G   (U)

   Explain:

4. Your savings from your summer job are in a savings account paying a fixed rate of interest.

   (H)   G   U

   Explain:

5. A widow lives entirely on income from fixed-rate corporate bonds.

   H   G   U

   Explain:

Activity written by Betty Shackelford, Maconaquah High School, Bunker Hill, Ind., and Kathleen Whitsett, Princeton High School, Cincinnati, Ohio.

6. A retired couple lives entirely on income from a pension the woman receives from her former employer.

   H   G   (U)

   Explain:

         Depends

7. A retired man lives entirely on income from Social Security.

   H   G   U

   Explain:

8. A retired bank official lives entirely on income from stock dividends.

   H   G   U

   Explain:

9. The federal government has a $5,000,000,000 debt.

   H   G   U

   Explain:

10. A firm signs a contract to provide maintenance services at a fixed rate for the next five years.

    H   G   U

    Explain:

11. A state government receives revenue mainly from a progressive income tax.

    H   G   U

    Explain:

12. A local government receives revenue mainly from fixed-rate license fees charged to businesses.

    H   G   U

    Explain:

13. Your friend rents an apartment with a three-year lease.

    H   G   U

    Explain:

14. A bank has loaned millions of dollars for home mortgages at a fixed rate of interest.

    H   G   U

    Explain:

15. Parents are putting savings for their child's college education in a bank savings account.

    H   G   U

    Explain:

16. What conclusions can you draw about who is helped and who is hurt by unanticipated inflation?

17. If you were certain that the inflation rate would be 10 percent a year for the next 10 years, how might your behavior change? Does your answer depend on who you are? Student? Worker?

Types of Unemployment

There are three types of unemployment:

■ *Frictional unemployment* includes people who are temporarily between jobs. They may have quit one job to find another, or they could be trying to find the best opportunity after graduating from high school or college.

■ *Cyclical unemployment* includes people who are not working because firms do not need their labor due to a lack of demand or a downturn in the business cycle. For example, if people are not buying many goods and services, workers are laid off.

■ *Structural unemployment* involves mismatches between job seekers and job openings. Unemployed people who lack skills or do not have sufficient education are structurally unemployed.

At full employment, we have frictional and structural unemployment, but cyclical unemployment would be zero. At full employment, the level of unemployment is called the *natural rate of unemployment*.

For each of the following situations, put the appropriate letter before the example.

F if it is an example of *frictional* unemployment.

C if it is an example of *cyclical* unemployment.

S if it is an example of *structural* unemployment.

___C___ 1. A computer programmer is laid off because of a recession.

___F___ 2. A literary editor leaves her job in New York to look for a new job in San Francisco.

___F___ 3. An unemployed college graduate is looking for his first job.

___S___ 4. Advances in technology make the assembly-line worker's job obsolete.

___C___ 5. Slumping sales lead to the cashier being laid off.

___S or F___ 6. An individual refuses to work for minimum wage.

___S___ 7. A high school graduate lacks the skills necessary for a particular job.

___C___ 8. Workers are laid off when the local manufacturing plant closes because the product made there isn't selling.

___S___ 9. A skilled glass blower becomes unemployed when a new machine does her job faster.

Activity written by John Morton, National Council on Economic Education, New York, N.Y., and James Spellicy, Lowell High School, San Francisco, Calif.

The Business Cycle

 Figure 17.1
The Business Cycle

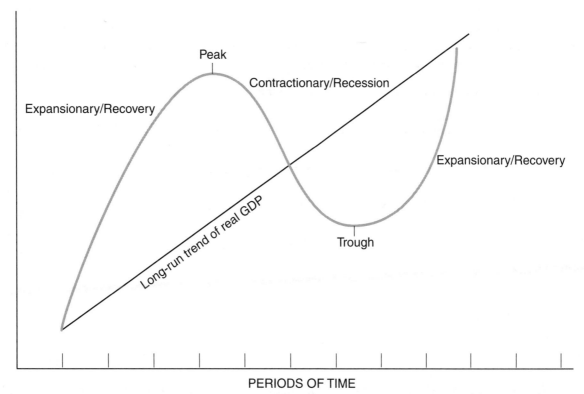

The curved line on Figure 17.1 shows a sample business cycle for an economy. The straight line represents the long-run trend of real GDP.

The business cycle can conveniently be divided into four phases:

1. **Expansionary or recovery phase.** Real output in the economy is increasing and the unemployment rate is declining. As the economic expansion continues, inflation may begin to accelerate.

2. **Peak.** Real output, GDP, is at its highest point of the business cycle.

3. **Contractionary or recession phase.** Real output in the economy is decreasing, and the unemployment rate is rising. As the contraction continues, inflationary pressures subside. If the recession continues long enough, prices may actually start to fall, a situation known as deflation.

4. **Trough.** The lowest point of real GDP reached during the business cycle is known as the trough. If the trough is particularly deep, it may be called a depression. A depression is an economic situation where the level of output falls to especially low levels and unemployment climbs to very high levels relative to the historical average. There is no precise decline in out-

Activity written by David Nelson, Western Washington University, Bellingham, Wash., with revision by Rae Jean B. Goodman, U.S. Naval Academy, Annapolis, Md.

put at which a serious recession becomes a depression. However, most business cycles do not end in a depression. The most recent depression the United States experienced was during the 1930s.

1. Figure 17.2 contains information for the U.S. economy from 1980 through 2001. For each quarter, first identify whether the economy was in an expansionary (E) or a contractionary (C) phase. Go back and pick out the quarters that correspond with a business cycle peak, and mark them with a P. Then find the quarters that correspond with a trough, and mark them with a T. Some of the answers have been provided for you.

Using your answers from Question 1, answer the following questions.

2. How many business cycles did the U.S. economy have between 1980 and 2001? _____

3. In how many quarters was output expanding? _____

4. In how many quarters was output contracting? _____

5. Which expansion looks best to you? Explain.

6. Which contraction looks worst to you? Explain.

7. During quarters in which real GDP fell, what happened to the unemployment rate compared with the previous quarter? Why?

8. Look at the unemployment rate in quarters corresponding to a business cycle peak. Why do you think there was still some unemployment in these quarters?

9. Look at the unemployment rate in quarters corresponding to recoveries. Why do you think the unemployment rate remained high?

10. Based on the years 1980 to 2001, how does the rate of inflation correspond with the business cycle?

Figure 17.2

The U.S. Economy from 1980

Year	Real GDP in 1996 Dollars (billions)	% Change From Previous Quarter	Civilian Unemployment Rate	Inflation Rate (CPI)	Phase of Business Cycle
1980q1	4,958.9	0.33	6.30	3.91	
1980q2	4,857.8	−2.04	7.32	3.67	
1980q3	4,850.3	−0.15	7.68	1.83	
1980q4	4,936.6	1.78	7.40	2.64	
1981q1	5,032.5	1.94	7.43	2.65	
1981q2	4,997.3	−0.70	7.40	2.32	
1981q3	5,056.8	1.19	7.42	2.82	
1981q4	4,997.1	−1.18	8.24	1.44	
1982q1	4,914.3	−1.66	8.84	0.82	
1982q2	4,935.5	0.43	9.43	1.52	
1982q3	4,912.1	−0.47	9.94	1.88	
1982q4	4,915.6	0.07	10.68	0.24	
1983q1	4,972.4	1.16	10.39	−0.07	
1983q2	5,089.8	2.36	10.10	1.26	
1983q3	5,180.4	1.78	9.36	1.18	
1983q4	5,286.8	2.05	8.54	0.90	
1984q1	5,402.3	2.18	7.87	1.12	E
1984q2	5,493.8	1.69	7.48	1.08	E
1984q3	5,541.3	0.86	7.45	1.10	E
1984q4	5,583.1	0.75	7.28	0.73	E
1985q1	5,629.7	0.83	7.28	0.63	E
1985q2	5,673.8	0.78	7.29	1.23	E
1985q3	5,758.6	1.49	7.21	0.71	E
1985q4	5,806.0	0.82	7.05	0.89	E
1986q1	5,858.9	0.91	7.02	0.21	E
1986q2	5,883.3	0.42	7.18	−0.21	E
1986q3	5,937.9	0.93	6.99	0.73	E
1986q4	5,969.5	0.53	6.83	0.55	E
1987q1	6,013.3	0.73	6.62	1.12	E

Figure 17.2 (continued)

Year	Real GDP in 1996 Dollars (billions)	% Change From Previous Quarter	Civilian Unemployment Rate	Inflation Rate (CPI)	Phase of Business Cycle
1987q2	6,077.2	1.06	6.28	1.31	E
1987q3	6,128.1	0.84	6.01	1.15	E
1987q4	6,234.4	1.73	5.87	0.84	E
1988q1	6,275.9	0.67	5.73	0.61	E
1988q2	6,349.8	1.18	5.49	1.26	E
1988q3	6,382.3	0.51	5.49	1.33	E
1988q4	6,465.2	1.30	5.35	1.04	
1989q1	6,543.8	1.22	5.22	1.11	
1989q2	6,579.4	0.54	5.24	1.64	
1989q3	6,610.6	0.47	5.28	0.81	
1989q4	6,633.5	0.35	5.37	0.96	
1990q1	6,716.3	1.25	5.30	1.72	
1990q2	6,731.7	0.23	5.34	1.02	
1990q3	6,719.4	−0.18	5.69	1.73	
1990q4	6,664.2	−0.82	6.11	1.62	
1991q1	6,631.4	−0.49	6.57	0.82	
1991q2	6,668.5	0.56	6.82	0.59	
1991q3	6,684.9	0.25	6.85	0.79	
1991q4	6,720.9	0.54	7.10	0.76	E
1992q1	6,783.3	0.93	7.38	0.70	E
1992q2	6,846.8	0.94	7.60	0.82	E
1992q3	6,899.7	0.77	7.63	0.79	E
1992q4	6,990.6	1.32	7.41	0.71	E
1993q1	6,988.7	−0.03	7.15	0.85	C
1993q2	7,031.2	0.61	7.07	0.77	E
1993q3	7,062.0	0.44	6.80	0.39	E
1993q4	7,168.7	1.51	6.62	0.69	E
1994q1	7,229.4	0.85	6.56	0.64	E
1994q2	7,330.2	1.39	6.17	0.64	E
1994q3	7,370.2	0.55	6.00	0.88	E

Figure 17.2 (continued)

Year	Real GDP in 1996 Dollars (billions)	% Change From Previous Quarter	Civilian Unemployment Rate	Inflation Rate (CPI)	Phase of Business Cycle
1994q4	7,461.1	1.23	5.62	0.47	E
1995q1	7,488.7	0.37	5.48	0.82	E
1995q2	7,503.3	0.19	5.68	0.88	E
1995q3	7,561.4	0.77	5.66	0.44	E
1995q4	7,621.9	0.80	5.57	0.48	E
1996q1	7,676.4	0.72	5.55	0.91	E
1996q2	7,802.9	1.65	5.47	0.99	E
1996q3	7,841.9	0.50	5.26	0.53	E
1996q4	7,931.3	1.14	5.31	0.72	E
1997q1	8,016.4	1.07	5.23	0.67	E
1997q2	8,131.9	1.44	4.98	0.40	E
1997q3	8,216.6	1.04	4.86	0.40	E
1997q4	8,272.9	0.69	4.68	0.39	E
1998q1	8,396.3	1.49	4.64	0.27	E
1998q2	8,442.9	0.56	4.42	0.54	E
1998q3	8,528.5	1.01	4.53	0.39	E
1998q4	8,667.9	1.63	4.43	0.35	E
1999q1	8,733.5	0.76	4.26	0.39	E
1999q2	8,771.2	0.43	4.26	0.97	E
1999q3	8,871.5	1.14	4.25	0.62	E
1999q4	9,049.9	2.01	4.10	0.62	E
2000q1	9,102.5	0.58	4.02	0.99	E
2000q2	9,229.4	1.39	4.00	1.06	E
2000q3	9,260.1	0.33	4.06	0.80	E
2000q4	9,303.9	0.47	3.97	0.54	E
2001q1	9,334.5	0.33	4.19	0.96	E
2001q2	9,341.7	0.08	4.47	1.04	E

Test Your Understanding of Macroeconomic Indicators

Answer the questions and briefly explain your answers.

1. The unemployment rate and employment both go up. Ellen says that it is not possible for both to rise at the same time. Is Ellen correct or incorrect? Why?

2. True, false or uncertain, and explain why? "Gross domestic product measures the amount of wealth in the economy."

3. True, false or uncertain, and explain why? "A decrease in gross domestic product must reduce a person's standard of living."

4. True, false or uncertain, and explain why? "If nominal GDP increases by 5 percent and the price level increases by 7 percent, real GDP has decreased."

5. True, false or uncertain, and explain why? "In preparing an index of prices, it is important that all commodities entering the index be given equal weight."

6. True, false or uncertain, and explain why? "*Frictional* and *structural* unemployment are two words for the same thing."

Several questions come from Phillip Saunders, *Introduction to Macroeconomics: Student Workbook,* 18th ed. (Bloomington, Ind., 1998). Copyright 1998 Phillip Saunders. All rights reserved. Betty Shackleford, Maconaquah High School, Bunker Hill, Ind., and Kathleen Whitsett, Princeton High School, Cincinnati, Ohio, contributed to this activity.

7. Why does unanticipated inflation help borrowers and hurt lenders?

8. True, false or uncertain, and explain why? "Inflation always increases when unemployment decreases."

9. True, false or uncertain, and explain why? "If the economy is at full employment, the unemployment rate is zero."

10. True, false or uncertain, and explain why? "Seasonal unemployment is a continual worry because some people are out of work on a regular basis."

Sample Multiple-Choice Questions

Circle the letter of each correct answer.

1. In the circular flow diagram, which of the following is true in the product market?

   (A) Households sell goods and services to business firms.

   (B) Households sell resources to business firms.

   (C) Business firms sell resources to households.

   (D) Business firms sell goods and services to households.

   (E) Households buy resources from business firms.

2. In the circular flow diagram, which of the following is true in resource or factor markets?

   (A) Households buy resources from business firms.

   (B) Households sell products to business firms.

   (C) Households sell resources to business firms.

   (D) Business firms sell goods and services to households.

   (E) Business firms sell resources to households.

3. Which of the following is the best measure of the production or output of an economy?

   (A) Consumer price index

   (B) Unemployment rate

   (C) Gross domestic product

   (D) Prime rate

   (E) Index of leading indicators

4. The market value of all final goods and services produced in the economy in a given year is

   (A) net national product.

   (B) national income.

   (C) personal income.

   (D) gross domestic product.

   (E) producer price index.

5. Which of the following people would be considered unemployed?

   (A) A person who quits work to care for aging parents

   (B) A person who stayed home to raise his children and now starts looking for a job

   (C) A person who quits a job to return to school full time

   (D) A person who is qualified to teach but is driving a bus until a teaching job is available

   (E) A person who works two part-time jobs but is looking for a full-time job

6. In the gross domestic product, the largest dollar amount is

   (A) consumer spending.

   (B) rental payments.

   (C) net exports of goods and services.

   (D) gross private domestic investment.

   (E) government purchases of goods and services.

7. The largest dollar amount of gross domestic product is

   (A) rental payments.

   (B) government expenditures on goods and services.

   (C) profit.

   (D) net interest.

   (E) wages and salaries to employees.

8. Which of the following purchases is included in the calculation of gross domestic product?

(A) A used economics textbook from the bookstore

(B) New harvesting equipment for the farm

(C) 1,000 shares of stock in a computer firm

(D) A car produced in a foreign country

(E) Government bonds issued by a foreign firm

9. Which of the following would be included in the calculation of gross domestic product?

(A) Government purchase of a new submarine

(B) Social Security payment to a retired military officer

(C) The purchase of a home built 10 years ago

(D) Contributions to a charity organization

(E) Work performed by a barber who cuts the hair of his or her own children

10. Which of the following would be counted as investment when calculating gross domestic product?

(A) The purchase of a used computer by an auto manufacturer

(B) The purchase of a share of IBM stock by an employee

(C) The construction of a new house

(D) The construction of roads by the government

(E) The profit earned when selling shares of stock

11. Which of the following would be an example of an *intermediate* good or service?

(A) A calculator purchased by a college student for taking exams

(B) Gasoline purchased by an insurance agent to visit clients at their homes

(C) A house purchased by a family with four children

(D) A car purchased by a student's parents and given to the student

(E) Tuition paid by a student at a state university

12. Of the following, which is the best example of *structural* unemployment?

(A) A computer programmer who quits her job to move to a warmer climate

(B) A construction worker who loses his job in the winter

(C) An auto worker who loses her job during a recession

(D) A steel worker who is replaced by a robot

(E) A toy maker who worked for a company that closed because consumers did not buy its toys

13. If the price index in a country were 100 for the year 2000 and 120 for 2003 and nominal gross domestic product in 2003 were $480 billion, then real gross domestic product for 2003 in 2000 dollars would be

(A) about $360 billion.

(B) about $380 billion.

(C) about $400 billion.

(D) about $600 billion.

(E) indeterminate with the given information.

Use the following information for a hypothetical economy to answer questions 14 and 15.

YEAR	Current or Nominal GDP	GDP Price Deflator Index (1990 = 100)	GDP Price Deflator Index (2000 = 100)
1990	$500	100	
2000	$1,200	200	100

14. The value of the gross domestic product in 2000, in terms of 1990 prices, was

   (A) $600.   (B) $700.

   (C) $1,000.   (D) $1,200.

   (E) $1,300.

15. If 2000 were made the base year for the GDP price deflator index, the value of the index number for 1990 (rounded to the nearest whole number) would be

   (A) zero.   (B) 42.

   (C) 142.   (D) 212.

   (E) 256.

16. The CPI tends to overstate true changes in the cost of living for which of the following reasons?
   I.   The index does not take into account a change in quality.
   II. Consumers change purchase patterns as prices change.
   III. The CPI includes only domestically produced goods.
   IV. Consumers often buy at discount rather than retail.

   (A) I only

   (B) I and II only

   (C) I, II and III only

   (D) I, II and IV only

   (E) I, II, III and IV

17. Which of the following is true about the natural rate of unemployment?

   (A) It can vary over time.

   (B) It is 2 percent or less of the civilian labor force.

   (C) It is equal to the structural unemployment rate.

   (D) It allows for some frictional and cyclical unemployment.

   (E) It is the full-employment rate minus the cyclical unemployment rate.

18. Suppose a factory added $5,000 worth of output this year. Incidentally, the waste from this factory caused $1,000 worth of loss to the neighboring waterways. As a result, gross domestic product will

   (A) increase by $5,000.

   (B) increase by $4,000.

   (C) increase by $1,000.

   (D) decrease by $4,000.

   (E) decrease by $1,000.

19. Which of the following is true if real GDP in Year 1 is $5,000 and in Year 2 is $5,200?

   (A) Output has increased by 4 percent.

   (B) Output has declined by 4 percent.

   (C) Output change is uncertain.

   (D) The economy is experiencing 4 percent inflation.

   (E) The economy is experiencing a recession.

20. When the actual inflation rate is greater than the anticipated inflation rate, which of the following is most likely to suffer?

   (A) Those who lend at a fixed interest rate

   (B) Those who borrow at a fixed interest rate

   (C) Retired persons with cost-of-living adjustment in their benefits

   (D) Employers who hire workers with long-term labor contracts

   (E) Those who lend with flexible interest rates

Sample Short Free-Response Questions

1. Answer the following questions about GDP.

   (A) Explain whether this statement is true, false or uncertain: "To ignore the production of intermediate goods when measuring the total product of a country means ignoring the work, the efforts and the incomes of millions of citizens. This is a mistake and can be rectified only by including intermediate goods production in GDP figures."

   (B) Give two reasons for using real GDP per capita as a measure of the standard of living for a nation.

   (C) Give two reasons why real GDP per capita is not a good measure of the standard of living for a nation.

2. Explain the statement "A man diminishes GDP by marrying his cook."

3. You read the headline: "Real GDP Rises 3% This Year; Further Increases Likely Next Year, Economists Say."

    (A) What does this headline mean? Be specific.

    (B) Why do people care about the growth in real GDP?

    (C) What is the difference between real GDP and nominal GDP?

4. In a certain year, the annual unemployment rate was 6.1 percent. Define the term *unemployment rate*, and explain its meaning. What other information do you want to know before recommending a policy to reduce unemployment? Explain why you would want to know this information.

5. You read the following headline: "Inflation Rate at 1.1% — Lowest Rate in 2 Decades."

    (A) What is meant by *inflation*?

    (B) How did the statisticians arrive at 1.1 percent? What measure did they probably use?

    (C) What does this headline imply about inflation during the previous 20 years?

6. The following table shows a price index for a five-year period.

   (A) Using 2000 as the base year, calculate the price index for each year.

Year	Price Index (1999 = 100)	Price Index (2000 = 100)
1998	88	
1999	100	
2000	120	
2001	132	
2002	140	

   (B) If 2001 nominal GDP were $400 billion and 2002 nominal GDP were $420 billion, what was the growth rate for the economy from 2001 to 2002?

7. Assume the inflation rate is 2 percent. How is this rate measured, and what does this rate of inflation mean to the average citizen?

Sample Long Free-Response Questions

1. Define *unanticipated inflation*. How does unanticipated inflation affect lenders, borrowers, home-owners and the federal government?

2. You read the following information about the economy:

- Real GDP up 3 percent from a year ago

- Unemployment rate of 4.6 percent

- Consumer price index up 6 percent from a year ago

- Index of leading indicators up for the last six months

- Prime interest rate of 10 percent, up from 7 percent a year ago

(A) Explain what each of these economic indicators measures and the significance of the current data for the economy.

(B) These indicators should paint a picture of the entire economy. Describe this picture.

Macroeconomics | Unit 3

Aggregate Demand and Aggregate Supply: Fluctuations in Outputs and Prices

(one of the most difficult units according to Mr. Mclean)

$$MPC = \frac{\Delta consumption}{\Delta disposable\ income}$$

$$MPS = \frac{\Delta savings}{\Delta disposable\ income}$$

income / gov't spending:

$$\frac{1}{MPS}$$

tax multiplier:

$$-\frac{MPC}{MPS}$$

- The Keynesian aggregate expenditure model is a simple model of the economy and shows the multiplied effect that changes in government spending, taxes and investment can have on the economy.

- The marginal propensity to consume (MPC) is the additional consumption spending from an additional dollar of income. The marginal propensity to save (MPS) is the additional savings from an additional dollar of income.

- The marginal propensity to consume and the marginal propensity to save are related by MPC + MPS = 1. In the simple model, an additional dollar of income will either be consumed or saved.

- The multiplier is a number that shows the relationship between changes in autonomous spending and maximum changes in real gross domestic product (real GDP).

- In a simple model, the formula for calculating the multiplier is

$$\text{Income expenditure multiplier} = \frac{1}{1 - \text{MPC}} = \frac{1}{\text{MPS}}$$

- The multiplier effects result from subsequent rounds of induced spending that occur when autonomous spending changes.

- Investment and its response to changes in the interest rate are important in understanding the relationship between monetary policy and GDP.

- Aggregate demand (AD) and aggregate supply (AS) curves look and operate much like the supply and demand curves used in microeconomics. However, these macroeconomic AD and AS curves depict different concepts, and they change for different reasons than do microeconomic demand and supply curves. AD and AS curves can be used to illustrate changes in real output and the price level of an economy.

- The downward sloping aggregate demand curve is explained by the interest rate effect, the wealth effect and the net export effect. The wealth effect is also called the real-balance effect.

- The aggregate supply curve can be divided into three ranges: the horizontal range, the upward sloping or intermediate range, and the vertical range.

- Shifts in aggregate demand can change the level of output, the price level or both. The determinants of aggregate demand include consumer spending, investment spending, government spending, net export spending and money supply.

- Shifts in aggregate supply can also change the level of output and the price level. The determinants of AS include changes in input prices, productivity, the legal institutional environment and the quantity of available resources.

- In the short run, economists think that equilibrium levels of GDP can occur at less than, greater than or at the full-employment level of GDP. Economists believe that long-run equilibrium can occur only at full employment.

- In a dynamic aggregate demand and aggregate supply model of the economy, changes in wages and prices over time induce the economy to move to the long-run equilibrium.

- Fiscal policy consists of government actions that may increase or decrease aggregate demand. These actions involve changes in government expenditures and taxation.

- The government uses an expansionary fiscal policy to try to increase aggregate demand during a recession. The government may decrease taxes, increase spending or do a combination of the two.

The government uses a contractionary fiscal policy to try to decrease aggregate demand when the economy is overheating. The government may increase taxes, decrease spending or do a combination of the two.

A change in output can also be illustrated by the Keynesian aggregate expenditure model. This model differs from the AD and AS model because in the Keynesian model the price level is assumed to be constant.

The AD and AS model can be reconciled with the Keynesian expenditure model. In the horizontal range of the AS curve, both models are identical. The models differ in the intermediate and vertical ranges of the AS curve.

Autonomous spending is that part of AD that is independent of the current rate of economic activity.

Induced spending is that part of AD that depends on the current level of economic activity.

Discretionary fiscal policy means the federal government must take deliberate action or pass a new law changing taxes or spending. The automatic or built-in stabilizers change government spending or taxes without new laws being passed or deliberate action being taken.

Stagflation, when the economy simultaneously experiences inflation and unemployment, can be explained by a decrease in aggregate supply.

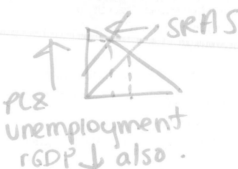

Keynesian Equilibrium

This activity is designed to give you practice with manipulations of the aggregate expenditure model. It shows you how the expenditure schedule is derived and how it helps to determine the equilibrium level of income. This activity assumes that the price level is constant with the consumer price index or price level having a value of 100. All numbers in Figure 19.1 are in billions of constant dollars.

 Figure 19.1
Income-Expenditure Schedule

Income (Output)	Consumption Spending	Investment Spending	Government Spending	Total Spending (Aggregate Expenditure)
$2,400	$2,500	$300	$100	
2,600	2,600	300	100	
2,800	2,700	300	100	
3,000	2,800	300	100	
3,200	2,900	300	100	
3,400	3,000	300	100	
3,600	3,100	300	100	
3,800	3,200	300	100	

1. Use the data on consumption spending and income to draw the consumption function on the graph in Figure 19.2. Label the function C.

2. Using the consumption function you have just drawn and the data on investment and government spending, draw the aggregate expenditure schedule on the same graph. Label it AE (C + I + G). What is the difference between the aggregate expenditure schedule and the consumption function?

3. Now draw a line representing all the points at which total spending and income could be equal. Label this the 45° line.

4. The 45° line represents all the points that *could be* the equilibrium level of total spending. Now circle the one point that *is* the equilibrium level of total spending. What is the equilibrium level of total spending on your graph? _____

Adapted from William J. Baumol and Alan S. Blinder, *Economics, Principles and Policy,* 3rd ed. (New York: Harcourt Brace & Company, 1985), p. 55. James Chasey, Homewood-Flossmoor High School, Flossmoor, Ill., contributed to this activity.

✳ Figure 19.2
Aggregate Expenditure Model

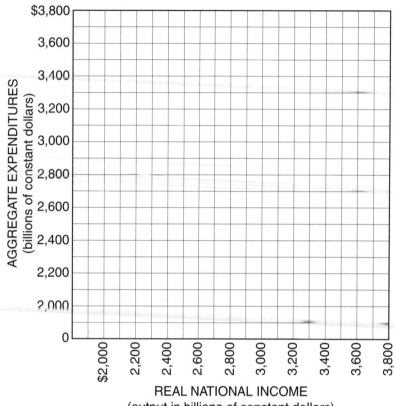

5. Based on the data in Figure 19.1, and assuming that the full-employment level of total spending is $3,600 billion, what conclusions can you draw about the equilibrium level of total spending?

6. Based on the data in Figure 19.1, and assuming that the full-employment level of total spending is $3,200 billion, what conclusions can you draw about the equilibrium level of total spending?

7. If government spending increased by $100 billion, what would be the new equilibrium level of total spending? _____ For the increase of $100 billion in government spending, total spending increased by _____. Explain why this occurs.

Practice with APC, APS, MPC and MPS

Part A
Average Propensities

The *average propensity to consume* (APC) is the ratio of consumption expenditures (C) to disposable income (DI), or APC = C / DI.

The *average propensity to save* (APS) is the ratio of savings (S) to disposable income, or APS = S / DI.

1. Using the data in Figure 20.1, calculate the APC and APS at each level of disposable income given. The first calculation is completed as an example.

Figure 20.1

Average Propensities to Consume and to Save

Disposable Income	Consumption	Saving	APC	APS
$0	$2,000	–$2,000	—	—
2,000	3,600	–1,600	1.8	–0.8
4,000	5,200	–1,200		
6,000	6,800	–800		
8,000	8,400	–400		
10,000	10,000	0		
12,000	11,600	400		

2. How can savings be negative? Explain.

Part B
Marginal Propensities

The *marginal propensity to consume* (MPC) is the change in consumption divided by the change in disposable income. It is a fraction of any change in DI that is spent on consumer goods: MPC = ΔC / ΔDI.

The *marginal propensity to save* (MPS) is the fraction saved of any change in disposable income. The MPS is equal to the change in saving divided by the change in DI: MPS = ΔS / ΔDI.

3. Using the data in Figure 20.2, calculate the MPC and MPS at each level of disposable income. The first calculation is completed as an example. (This is not a typical consumption function. Its purpose is to provide practice in calculating MPC and MPS.)

Activity written by John Morton, National Council on Economic Education, New York, N.Y., and James Spellicy, Lowell High School, San Francisco, Calif.

✳ Figure 20.2
Marginal Propensities to Consume and to Save

Disposable Income	Consumption	Saving	MPC	MPS
$12,000	$12,100	−$100	—	—
13,000	13,000	0	0.90	0.10
14,000	13,800	200		
15,000	14,500	500		
16,000	15,100	900		
17,000	15,600	1,400		

4. Why must the sum of MPC and MPS always equal 1?

Part C

✳ Figure 20.3
Changes in APC and MPC as DI Increases

Disposable Income	Consumption	Savings	APC	APS	MPC	MPS
$10,000	$12,000	−$2,000			—	—
20,000	21,000	−1,000				
30,000	30,000	0				
40,000	39,000	1,000				
50,000	48,000	2,000				
60,000	57,000	3,000				
70,000	66,000					

5. Complete Figure 20.3, and answer the questions based on the completed table.

6. What is the APC at a DI level of $10,000? _____ At $20,000? _____

7. What happens to the APC as DI rises? _____

8. What is the MPC as DI goes from $50,000 to $60,000? _____ From $60,000 to $70,000? _____

9. What happens to MPC as income rises? _____ What happens to MPS as income rises? _____

10. What is the conceptual difference between APC and MPC?

The Magic of the Multiplier

The people in Econoland live on an isolated island. One year a stranger arrived and built a factory to make seashell charms. The factory is considered an investment on Econoland. If the marginal propensity to consume on the island were 75 percent, or 0.75, this would mean that Econoland residents would consume or spend 75 percent of any change in income and save 25 percent of any change in income. The additional spending would generate additional income and eventually a multiple increase in income. This is called the *multiplier effect.* When they heard about this multiplier effect, the islanders were thrilled about the new factory because they liked the idea of additional income.

The residents of Econoland wanted to know what would eventually happen to the levels of GDP, consumption and saving on the island as the new spending worked its way through the economy. Luckily there was a retired university economist who had settled on Econoland who offered a brief statement of the multiplier. "It's simple," he said: **"One person's spending becomes another person's income."** The economist began a numerical example. "This shows the process," he said. The rounds refer to the new spending moving from resident to resident. He stopped his example at four rounds and added the rest of the rounds to cover all Econoland's citizens.

Figure 21.1

Changes in Econoland's GDP, Consumption and Saving

Round	Income (GDP)	Consumption Spending	Saving
Round 1	$1,000	0.75 of $1,000 = $750	0.25 of $1,000 = $250
Round 2	One person's spending becoming another person's income: $750	0.75 of $750 = $562.50	0.25 of $750 = $187.50
Round 3	The next person's spending becoming another person's income: $562.50	0.75 of $562.50 = $421.88	0.25 of $562.50 = $140.62
Round 4	The next person's spending becoming another person's income: $421.87	0.75 of $421.88 = $316.41	0.25 of $421.87 = $105.47
Rounds continue	. . .	. . .	. . .
All rounds	**Final outcome for income (GDP)** **1 / (1 – 0.75) x $1,000 = 4 x $1,000 = $4,000**	**Final outcome for consumption spending** **0.75 of $4,000 = $3,000**	**Final outcome for saving** **0.25 of $4,000 = $1,000**

Activity written by Charles Bennett, Gannon University, Erie, Pa.

The retired economist then summarized the multiplier effect for the assembled crowd of Econolanders. "This shows us that the factory is an investment that has a multiplied effect on our GDP. In this case, the multiplier is 4." He added, "It appears to be magic, but it is simply that *one person's spending becomes another person's income.*" There were some nods of agreement but also many puzzled looks, so the old professor asked the citizens a series of questions. Answer these questions as if you were an Econolander.

1. Would the multiplier be larger or smaller if you saved more of your additional income? _____

2. What do you think would happen if all Econolanders saved all of the change in their incomes?

3. What would happen if you spent *all* of the change in your income?

The professor broke out into a smile as the answers all came out correct.

The economist reminded the islanders about the multiplied effect on GDP that a new road around the island would have. That new bridge built by the island government over the lagoon would also have a multiplied effect on GDP. This time there were many more nods of approval and understanding.

The economist also indicated that if the government of Econoland lowered taxes, the citizens would have more income to spend, which would cause a multiplier effect. He said there was another side to this: If the taxes were raised, there would be a multiplier effect, which would decrease income and GDP by a multiple amount.

The King of Econoland commissioned the old economist to write a simple explanation about multipliers so all the citizens of Econoland would understand. He told the old economist: "If you succeed in helping all citizens understand the multiplier in simple terms, you will be rewarded. If not, you will be banished from the island."

The economist started banging away on an old rusting typewriter since he did not want to be banished from this island paradise. The result follows:

The Professor's Treatise on Multipliers

MULTIPLIER FORMULAS AND TERMS

Marginal propensity to consume (MPC) = change in consumption divided by change in income

Marginal propensity to save (MPS) = change in saving divided by change in income

Investment Multiplier = 1 /(1 – MPC) or simply 1 /MPS

How to use the investment multiplier: change in GDP = change in investment times investment multiplier

When to use the investment multiplier: when there is a change in investment such as a new factory or new equipment

Government Spending Multiplier = 1 /(1 – MPC) or simply 1 /MPS

How to use the government spending multiplier: change in GDP = change in government spending times government spending multiplier

When to use the government spending multiplier: when there is a change in government spending such as a new road or bridge

Tax Multiplier = – MPC /(1 – MPC) = – MPC /MPS

How to use the tax multiplier: change in GDP = change in taxes times tax multiplier

When to use the tax multiplier: when there is a change in lump-sum taxes. Remember that the tax multiplier has a negative sign.

Figure 21.2

Multiplier Table
(Derived from using the formulas above)

MPC	Investment Multiplier	Government Spending Multiplier	Tax Multiplier
0.90	10.0	10.0	–9.0
0.80	5.0	5.0	–4.0
0.75	4.0	4.0	–3.0
0.60	2.5	2.5	–1.5
0.50	2.0	2.0	–1.0

"ALWAYS" RULES (A surefire way to remember multipliers)

The investment multiplier is *always* equal to the same value as the government spending multiplier.

The investment and government spending multipliers are *always* positive.

The tax multiplier is *always* negative.

The King took the treatise and had it printed for every islander. He then ordered the old professor to make up a series of questions to see if the subjects understood the multiplier.

Answer the questions on the professor's test.

The Econoland Test

1. What is the value of the tax multiplier if the MPC is 0.80? $\frac{-.8}{.2} = -4$

2. What is the value of the government spending multiplier if the MPC is 0.67? $\frac{1}{1-\frac{2}{3}} = \frac{1}{\frac{1}{3}} = 3$

3. What is the tax multiplier if the MPS is 0.25? $\frac{-.75}{1-.75} = \frac{-.75}{.25} = -3$

4. How could the multiplier be used to explain wide swings in income (which could be called business cycles) in Econoland?

   multiplier effect goes up and stronger means good and high things going on.

5. The numerical value for the investment and government spending multiplier increases as the
   ↓MPS↑MPC= ✓ (A) value of the marginal propensity to save decreases.
   (B) value of the average propensity to consume increases.
   (C) value of the marginal propensity to consume decreases.
   (D) value of the marginal propensity to save increases.
   (E) value of the average propensity to consume decreases.

6. If the government spending multiplier is 5 in Econoland, the value of the tax multiplier must be
   (A) 5
   (B) 4
   (C) 1
   (D) – 4
   (E) – 5

Macroeconomics • Mr. McLean

Econoland has the following values for income and consumption. Use this data to answer questions 7, 8 and 9.

Income	Consumption
100	150
200	225
300	300
400	375
500	450
600	525

7. The government spending multiplier in Econoland is

    (A) 3

    (B) 4

    (C) 5

    (D) 10

    (E) 30

$MPC = \dfrac{\Delta cons}{\Delta inc} = \dfrac{75}{100} = .75$

$MPS = 0.25$

8. If there is an increase in taxes of $200 in Econoland, the decrease in GDP will be

    (A) $100

    (B) $200

    (C) $400

    (D) $600

    (E) $800

9. If there is an increase in government spending of $100 and an increase in taxes of $100 in Econoland, then the change in GDP will be

    (A) $50

    (B) $100

    (C) $200

    (D) –$100

    (E) –$200

$100(4) = 400$

$100(-3) = -300$

$\overline{ \quad 100}$

10. Why do the people of Econoland need to understand multipliers?

    Econoland need to understand multipliers to see how the company is affected by using such.

Advanced Placement Macroeconomics

Investment Demand

Investment spending consists of spending on new buildings, machinery, plant and equipment. Investment spending is a part of total spending or aggregate expenditures. Any increase in investment spending would necessarily increase total spending or aggregate expenditures.

Decisions on investment spending are based on a comparison of marginal cost and marginal benefit: If you expect a particular project to yield a greater benefit than cost, you will undertake it. One of the costs associated with investment spending is the interest expense on borrowed money to engage in the project.

Part A

1. Figure 22.1 lists the expected cost of various projects and the associated expected benefit. Fill in the decision column with Yes if you would undertake the project and No if you would not. The first example has been completed for you.

 Figure 22.1

Comparison of Costs and Benefits of Different Projects

Cost	Benefit	Decision
$65	$20	No
$55	$30	
$45	$40	
$35	$50	
$25	$60	

2. If interest rates fell and the cost associated with the project fell by $15 at each level, indicate in Figure 22.2 which projects you would undertake. The first example has been completed for you.

 Figure 22.2

Comparison of Project Costs and Benefits with Decrease in Costs

Cost	Benefit	Decision
$50	$20	No
	$30	
	$40	
	$50	
	$60	

Activity written by James Chasey, Homewood-Flossmoor High School, Flossmoor, Ill.

Part B

Figure 22.3 lists the dollar value of investment projects that would be profitable at each interest rate.

 Figure 22.3

Country A and Country B Investment Data

Interest Rate	Country A Investment	Country B Investment
10%	$10	$70
8	50	75
6	90	80
4	130	85
2	170	90

 Figure 22.4

Investment Demand Curves

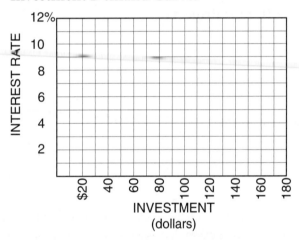

3. Plot the investment demand curve for Country A on Figure 22.4 and label it I_A.

4. Plot the investment demand curve for Country B on Figure 22.4, and label it I_B.

5. Which country would experience the larger increase in the amount of investment spending if interest rates in each country dropped from 8 percent to 6 percent?

6. How would you characterize the responsiveness of investment spending to the interest rates in Country A compared with Country B?

7. Assuming an MPC of 75 percent, what would be the effect on real GDP in Country A and Country B if real interest rates decline from 8 percent to 6 percent?

8. What conclusions can be reached about the elasticity of the investment demand curve and the effect a given change in interest rates would have on equilibrium real GDP?

9. Looking at the graph you drew, the investment demand curve is downward sloping in both Country A and Country B. Why does the investment demand curve have a downward slope?

Part C

Use Figure 22.5 to help answer questions 10, 11 and 12.

Figure 22.5

Shift in Investment Demand Curve

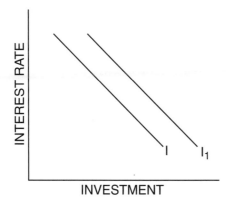

10. If interest rates rise, will the investment demand curve shift to a new location? If so, in what direction?

11. The shift in the investment demand curve shown in Figure 22.5 (I to I_1) represents a new location for the entire curve. How would you interpret the difference between movement along an existing investment demand curve and a shift in the location of the curve?

12. List two factors that could cause a shift in the investment demand curve as shown in Figure 22.5.

An Introduction to Aggregate Demand

Part A
Why Is the Aggregate Demand Curve Downward Sloping?

 Figure 23.1
Aggregate Demand Curve

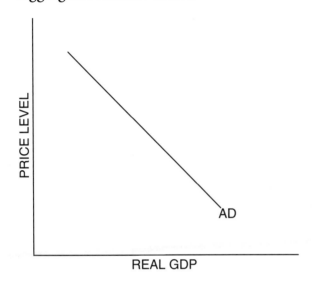

1. According to the AD curve, what is the relationship between the price level and real GDP?

2. Explain how each of the following effects helps explain why the AD curve is downward sloping.

   (A) Interest rate effect

   (B) Wealth effect or real-balance effect

   (C) Net export effect

Activity written by John Morton, National Council on Economic Education, New York, N.Y.

3. In what ways do the reasons that explain the downward slope of the AD curve differ from the reasons that explain the downward slope of the demand curve for a single product?

Part B
What Shifts the Aggregate Demand Curve?

Figure 23.2
Shifts in Aggregate Demand

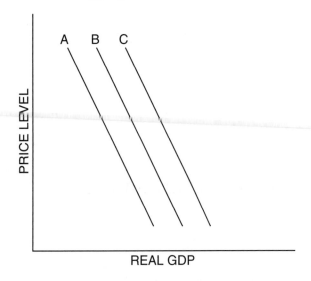

4. Using Figure 23.2, determine whether each situation below will cause an increase, decrease or no change in AD. Always start at curve B. If the situation would cause an increase in AD, draw an up arrow in column 1. If it causes a decrease, draw a down arrow. If there is no change, write NC. For each situation that causes a change in aggregate demand, write the letter of the new demand curve in column 2. Move only one curve.

Situation	1. Change in AD	2. New AD Curve
(A) Congress cuts taxes.		
(B) Autonomous investment spending decreased.		
(C) Government spending to increase next fiscal year; president promises no increase in taxes.		
(D) Survey shows consumer confidence jumps.		
(E) Stock market collapses; investors lose billions.		
(F) Productivity rises for fourth straight year.		
(G) President cuts defense spending by 20 percent; no increase in domestic spending.		

An Introduction to Short-Run Aggregate Supply

Part A
Why Can the Aggregate Supply Curve Have Three Different Shapes?

 Figure 24.1
Possible Shapes of Aggregate Supply Curve

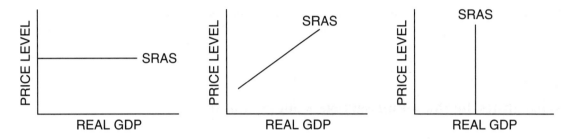

1. Under what conditions would an economy have a horizontal SRAS curve?

2. Under what conditions would an economy have a vertical SRAS curve?

3. Under what conditions would an economy have a positively sloped SRAS curve?

Activity written by John Morton, National Council on Economic Education, New York, N.Y.

---

4. Assume AD increased. What would be the effect on real GDP and the price level if the economy had a horizontal SRAS curve? A positively sloped SRAS curve? A vertical SRAS curve?

5. What range of the SRAS curve do you think the economy is in today? Explain.

Part B
What Shifts the Short-Run Aggregate Supply Curve?

✳ Figure 24.2
Shifts in Short-Run Aggregate Supply

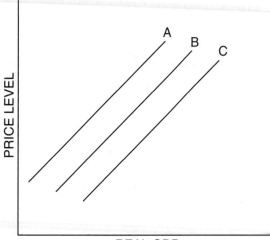

6. Using Figure 24.2, determine whether each situation below will cause an increase, decrease or no change in short-run aggregate supply (SRAS). Always start at curve B. If the situation would cause an increase in SRAS, draw an up arrow in column 1. If it causes a decrease, draw a down arrow. If there is no change, write NC. For each situation that causes a change in SRAS, write the letter of the new curve in column 2. Move only one curve.

Situation	1. Change in SRAS	2. New SRAS Curve
(A) Unions grow more aggressive; wage rates increase.		
(B) OPEC successfully increases oil prices.		
(C) Labor productivity increases dramatically.		
(D) Giant natural gas discovery decreases energy prices.		
(E) Computer technology brings new efficiency to industry.		
(F) Government spending increases.		
(G) Cuts in tax rates increase incentives to save.		
(H) Low birth rate will decrease the labor force in future.		
(I) Research shows that improved schools have increased the skills of American workers and managers.		

Short-Run Equilibrium Price Level and Output

Part A
Equilibrium

 Figure 25.1
Equilibrium Price and Output Levels

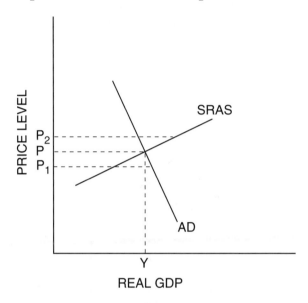

1. What are the equilibrium price level and output? _____

2. What would eventually happen to the price level and output if the initial price level were P$_2$ rather than P? Why would this happen?

3. What would eventually happen to the price level and output if the initial price level were P$_1$ rather than P? Why would this happen?

Activity written by John Morton, National Council on Economic Education, New York, N.Y., and James Stanley, Choate Rosemary Hall, Wallingford, Conn.

Part B
Changes in the Equilibrium Price Level and Output

For each situation described below, illustrate the change on the AD and AS graph and describe the effect on the equilibrium price level and real GDP by circling the correct symbol: ↑ for increase, ↓ for decrease, or — for unchanged.

4. Congress passes a tax cut for the middle class, and the president signs it.

Middle Class Tax Cut

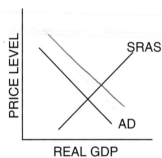

Price level: ↑ ↓ —

Real GDP: ↑ ↓ —

5. During a recession, the government increases spending on schools, highways and other public works.

Increased Government Spending

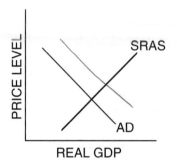

Price level: ↑ ↓ —

Real GDP: ↑ ↓ —

6. New oil discoveries cause large decreases in energy prices.

New Oil Discoveries

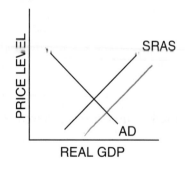

Price level ↑ ↓ —

Real GDP ↑ ↓ —

7. Illustrate the effects of an increase in aggregate demand.

Effects of an Increase in AD

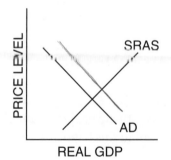

Price level ↑ ↓ —

Real GDP ↑ ↓ —

8. Illustrate the effects of increases in production costs.

Effects of Increases in Production Costs

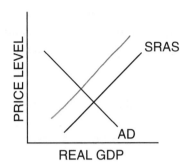

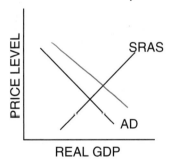

| Price level | ↑ | ↓ | — |
| Real GDP | ↑ | ↓ | — |

9. New technology and better education increase productivity.

Effects of New Technology and Better Education

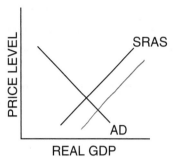

| Price level | ↑ | ↓ | — |
| Real GDP | ↑ | ↓ | — |

10. A new president makes consumers and businesses more confident about the future economy. **Note:** Show the change in AD only.

Increased Confidence for Future Economy

| Price level | ↑ | ↓ | — |
| Real GDP | ↑ | ↓ | — |

11. With the unemployment rate at five percent, the federal government reduces personal taxes and increases spending. **Note:** Show the change in AD only.

Reduced Taxes and Increased Government Spending

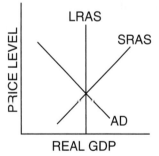

| Price level | ↑ | ↓ | — |
| Real GDP | ↑ | ↓ | — |

Part C
Summarizing Aggregate Demand and Aggregate Supply Shifts

For each of the events below, make additions to the graph to illustrate the change. Then indicate the response in terms of shifts in or movements along the aggregate demand or aggregate supply curve and the short-run effect on real GDP and the price level. Indicate *shifts* in the curve by S and movements *along* the curve by A. Indicate the changes in price level, unemployment and real GDP with an up arrow for an increase and a down arrow for a decrease.

	1. Increase in labor productivity due to technological change	2. Increase in the price of inputs used by many firms	3. Boom in investment assuming some unemployed resources are available	4. A major reduction in investment spending
	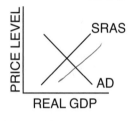			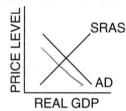
AD Curve	—	—	—	↓
AS Curve	↑	↓	↑	—
Real GDP	↑	↓	↑	↓
Price Level	↓	↑	↑	↓
Unemployment	↓	↑	↓	↑

Reconciling the Keynesian Aggregate Expenditure Model With the Aggregate Demand and Aggregate Supply Model

Now it is time to reconcile the Keynesian aggregate expenditure model with the aggregate demand and supply model. We find both differences and similarities when comparing the two models:

■ The Keynesian model is a fixed, or constant, price model while the AD and AS model is a variable-price model. The vertical axis of the Keynesian model is *aggregate expenditure* while the vertical axis of the AD and AS model is *price level*.

"CIGNET"

■ Aggregate expenditure (C + I + G + Net Exports) on the Keynesian model is aggregate demand on the AD and AS model. A shift upward in aggregate expenditure is the same as a shift outward in aggregate demand. A shift downward of aggregate expenditure is the same as a shift inward of aggregate demand.

■ The AD and AS model can account for shifts in aggregate supply. The Keynesian model cannot do so.

■ In the Keynesian model, a shift in aggregate expenditures results in the full multiplier effect, and the multiplier can easily be calculated from the graphs. In the AD and AS model, the multiplier is not at full strength on the positively sloped and vertical AS curves.

■ In the AD and AS model, the increase in the price level diminishes the impact of the multiplier.

Activity written by John Morton, National Council on Economic Education, New York, N.Y.

For each of the following situations, illustrate the indicated change on both the AD and AS model and the Keynesian model.

1. The economy is at less than *full* employment. An increase in consumer confidence moves the economy to *full* employment.

 Figure 26.1

An Increase in Consumer Confidence

Less Than Full Employment
Using the AD and AS Model

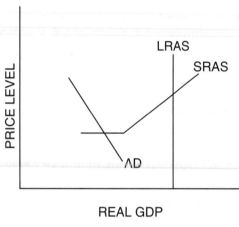

Less Than Full Employment
Using the Keynesian Model

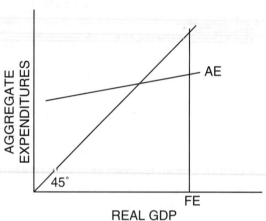

2. The economy is at full employment but businesses begin to believe that a recession is ahead.

 Figure 26.2

Businesses Believe a Recession Is Coming

Full Employment
Using the AD and AS Model

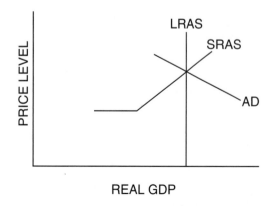

Full Employment
Using the Keynesian Model

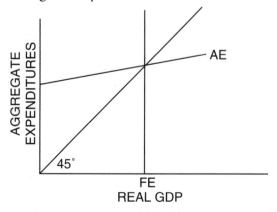

Manipulating the AD and AS Model: Exogenous Demand and Supply Shocks

Part A
Exogenous Demand Shocks

An *exogenous demand shock* is a change in an exogenous variable — a variable determined outside the model — that affects aggregate demand. Read the description of each exogenous demand shock, and then draw a new AD curve that will represent the change the demand shock caused. Label the new curve AD_1. Then briefly explain the reason for the change in the graph.

1. **Exogenous Demand Shock:** Economic booms in both Japan and Europe result in massive increases in orders for exported goods from the United States.

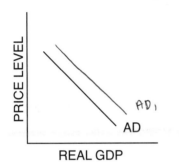

EXPLANATION:

$X\uparrow \rightarrow \uparrow NX \rightarrow \uparrow AD$

2. **Exogenous Demand Shock:** As part of its countercyclical policy, the government both reduces taxes and increases transfer payments.

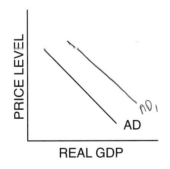

EXPLANATION:

$\downarrow$ Taxes and $\uparrow$ Transfers $\rightarrow \uparrow$ disposable income
$\rightarrow \uparrow C \uparrow I \rightarrow \uparrow AD$

Activity written by Robert Nuxoll, Oceanside High School, Oceanside, N.Y.

3. **Exogenous Demand Shock:** While the United States was in the midst of the Great Depression, a foreign power attacked, Congress declared war and more than 1,000,000 soldiers were drafted in the first year while defense spending was increased several times over.

EXPLANATION:

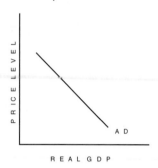

4. **Exogenous Demand Shock:** To balance the budget, the federal government cuts Social Security payments by 10 percent and federal aid to education by 20 percent.

EXPLANATION:

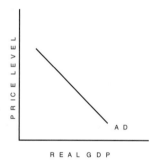

Part B
Exogenous Supply Shocks

The cause of an *exogenous supply shock* is the change in an exogenous variable — a variable determined outside the model — that affects aggregate supply. Read the description of each exogenous shock to short-run aggregate supply, and then draw a new SRAS curve that will represent the change caused by the shock. Label the new curve SRAS$_1$. Then briefly explain the reason for the change in the graph.

5. **Exogenous Supply Shock**: New environmental standards raise the average cost of autos and trucks 5 percent.

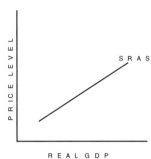

EXPLANATION:

6. **Exogenous Supply Shock**: Fine weather results in the highest corn and wheat yields in 40 years.

EXPLANATION:

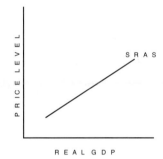

7. **Exogenous Supply Shock**: Because of decreased international tension, the government sells off thousands of army-surplus Jeeps and trucks at prices that are far less than the market price for their commercial counterparts.

EXPLANATION:

8. **Exogenous Supply Shock:** An enemy power sets up a blockade of the sea lanes leading to a country, and most ships refuse to deliver cargo through the blockade.

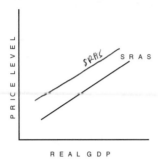

EXPLANATION:

Goods to mkt ↓ → ↓ SRAS

Part C
Manipulating the Aggregate Supply and Demand Model

Read each of the scenarios below, and explain the impact the exogenous shocks will have on short-run aggregate supply and aggregate demand. Then draw a correctly labeled aggregate demand and aggregate supply graph to illustrate each short-run impact.

9. During a long, slow recovery from a recession, consumers postponed major purchases. Suddenly they begin to buy cars, refrigerators, televisions and furnaces to replace their failing models.

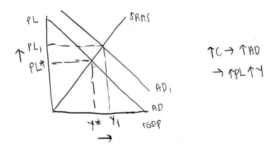

↑C → ↑AD
→ ↑PL ↑Y

10. With no other dramatic changes, the government raises taxes and reduces transfer payments in the hope of balancing the federal budget.

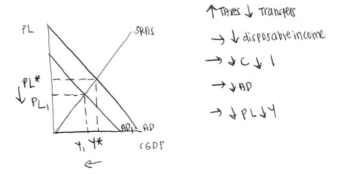

↑ Taxes ↓ Transfers
→ ↓ disposable income
→ ↓C ↓I
→ ↓AD
→ ↓PL ↓Y

11. News of possible future layoffs frightens the public into reducing spending and increasing saving for the feared "rainy day."

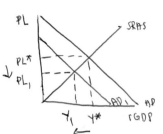

$\downarrow C \rightarrow \downarrow AD$

12. Because of rising tensions in many developing countries, firms begin to build new factories in Econoland and to purchase sophisticated machinery from Econoland businesses that will enable them to produce in Econoland at prices that are competitive.

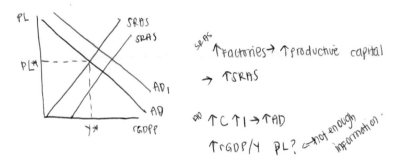

SRAS $\uparrow$ Factories $\rightarrow$ $\uparrow$ productive capital
$\rightarrow$ $\uparrow$ SRAS

AD $\uparrow C \uparrow I \rightarrow \uparrow AD$
$\uparrow$ rGDP/Y PL? $\leftarrow$ not enough information

13. Brazil solves its foreign debt and inflation problems. It then orders $10 billion worth of capital machinery from Econoland. Draw the AD and short-run AS graph for Econoland.

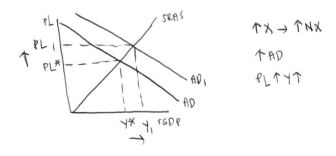

$\uparrow X \rightarrow \uparrow NX$
$\uparrow AD$
$PL \uparrow Y \uparrow$

IF I SHOULD LOVE AGAIN, IF I FIND SOMEONE NEW.
IT WOULD BE MAKE BELIEVE FOR IN MY HEART IT WOULD BE YOU.

The Macroeconomic Model: Short Run to Long Run

In this activity we are working from the short run to the long run. The aggregate demand curve is downward sloping and the aggregate supply curve is upward sloping. The aggregate supply curve is upward sloping in the short run because of slow wage and price adjustments within the economy.

Part A

1. In the following graph, suppose the aggregate demand shifts from AD to AD₁. How will the economy react over time? Assume that no monetary or fiscal policy is undertaken.

 Figure 28.1
Increase in Aggregate Demand
Starting at Full Employment

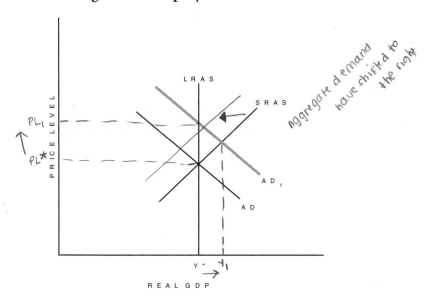

(A) What will happen to output in the short run? Explain.

PRODUCING ABOVE FULL EMPLOYMENT
Price LEVEL WILL ALSO GO UP.

(B) What will happen to output as the economy moves to the long-run equilibrium? Explain.

OUTPUT RETURN TO OUTPUT ★

BACK @ EQUILIBRIUM with a higher PL.

(C) What will happen to the price level? Explain.

PL↑ as firms pay higher wages

Activity written by Rae Jean B. Goodman, U.S. Naval Academy, Annapolis, Md. Part B was written by Robert Nuxoll, Oceanside High School, Oceanside, N.Y.

Sobra°°
mahal na mahal kita.°°
Hindi ako matatakot, mahihiya

GAGAWIN

(D) What will happen to wages? Explain.

wages will be driven up b/c of producing beyond Y* (overemployment)

(E) In the graph, draw the shifts in AD and SRAS that you think will occur. Indicate the final aggregate demand and short-run aggregate supply curves by labeling them as AD_f and $SRAS_f$.

Aggregate Demand remain @ AD₁

2. In the following graph, suppose the aggregate supply shifts from SRAS to SRAS₁. How will the economy react over time? Assume that no monetary or fiscal policy is undertaken.

Figure 28.2

Change in Short-Run Aggregate Supply

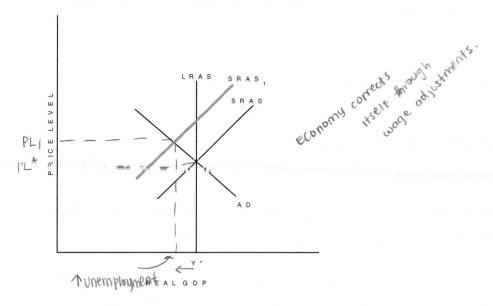

(A) What will happen to output in the short run? Explain.

It will decrease

(B) What will happen to output as the economy moves to the long-run equilibrium? Explain.

(C) What will happen to the price level? Explain.

(D) What will happen to wages? Explain.

↓

(E) In the graph, draw the shifts in AD and SRAS that you think will occur. Indicate the final aggregate demand and short-run aggregate supply curves by labeling them as AD_f and $SRAS_f$.

Part B

Read the description of each exogenous shock to aggregate supply and aggregate demand. Draw a new SRAS or AD curve that represents the change caused by the shock in the short run. Explain the reasons for the change in the graph, and then explain what happens in the long run if no stabilization policy is implemented. Identify the final AD curve as AD_f and the final SRAS curve as $SRAS_f$. If there is a change in LRAS, show the change and label the new curve $LRAS_f$.

3. The government increases defense spending by 10 percent a year over a five-year period.

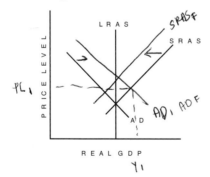

EXPLANATION:

↑ G → ↑ AD

4. OPEC cuts oil production by 30 percent, and the world price of oil rises by 40 percent.

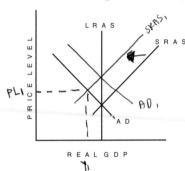

EXPLANATION:

5. The government increases spending on education, health care, housing and basic services for low-income people. No increase in taxes accompanies the program.

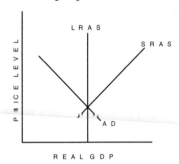

EXPLANATION:

6. Can the government maintain output above the natural level of output with aggregate demand policy? If the government attempts to, what will be the result?

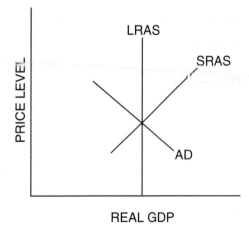

Long-Run Aggregate Supply (LRAS) and the Production Possibilities Curve (PPC)

The long-run aggregate supply (LRAS) curve differs from the short-run aggregate supply (SRAS) curve. The LRAS curve is a vertical line at an output level that represents the quantity of goods and services a nation can produce over a sustained period using all of its productive resources as efficiently as possible with all of the current technology available to it. Long-run aggregate supply is at full employment. LRAS doesn't change as the price level changes. Developing more and better resources or improving technology will shift the LRAS curve outward, but it will still be vertical.

The LRAS curve represents a point on an economy's production possibilities curve. Remember that the production possibilities curve (PPC) represents the maximum output of two goods that can be produced given scarce resources. The economy could grow if the PPC shifts outward because of more resources or technological advances. For the same reason, the LRAS curve shifts outward if more resources are developed or if there are technological advances.

SRAS can actually be greater than LRAS. Resources can be used more intensively in the short run. For example, workers can work more hours and machines can operate for more hours. However, this output level cannot be sustained in the long run. Eventually, the equilibrium level of output will fall unless LRAS is increased. As an analogy on a personal level, you may pull an all-nighter to prepare for several exams on the same day. You cannot, however, work 24 hours a day all the time.

Activity written by James Stanley, Choate Rosemary Hall, Wallingford, Conn.

Now answer the questions that follow to be sure you understand these concepts. Use the graphs in Figure 29.1 in your answers.

 Figure 29.1

Aggregate Supply and Production Possibilities Curves

LRAS and SRAS Curves

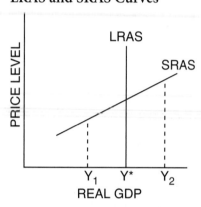

PPC Graph

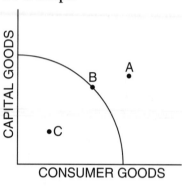

1. What information does a PPC provide for us about a nation's economy?

2. What assumptions do you make about the use of available resources when drawing a PPC?

3. What would cause a nation's PPC to shift?

4. What do you know about a nation's economy that is operating on the LRAS curve?

5. Under what conditions would an economy be on the LRAS curve?

6. If the price level rises, will LRAS shift? _____ Will the LRAS curve shift if AD changes? _____

7. If an economy finds that it faces a short-run equilibrium where real GDP is Y_1, how would you describe the condition of the economy? Given this equilibrium level of output, at what point would the economy lie on the PPC? Explain your answer.

8. If an economy finds that it faces a short-run equilibrium where real GDP is Y, how would you describe the condition of the economy? Given this equilibrium level of output, at what point would the economy lie on the PPC? Explain your answer.

9. If an economy finds that it faces a short-run equilibrium where real GDP is Y_2, how would you describe the condition of the economy? Given this equilibrium level of output, at what point would the economy lie on the PPC? Explain your answer.

10. If the economy were producing at Y_2, what would happen in the long run? Why?

11. What could cause a nation's LRAS to shift?

12. How would a rightward shift in LRAS be shown on the PPC?

The Tools of Fiscal Policy

Changes in federal taxes and federal government spending designed to affect the level of aggregate demand in the economy are called *fiscal policy*.

Aggregate demand is the total amount of spending on goods and services in the economy during a stated period of time. Aggregate demand consists of consumer spending, government spending, investment spending and net exports.

Aggregate supply consists of the total amount of goods and services available in the economy during a stated period of time.

During a recession, aggregate demand is usually too low to bring about full employment of resources. Government can increase aggregate demand by spending more, cutting taxes or doing both. These actions often result in budget deficits because the government spends more than it collects in taxes. Increasing government spending without increasing taxes or decreasing taxes without decreasing government expenditures should increase aggregate demand. Such an *expansionary fiscal policy* should increase employment, the price level or both.

If the level of aggregate demand is too high, creating inflationary pressure, government can reduce its spending, increase taxes or do both. These actions should result in a larger budget surplus or a smaller budget deficit than existed before. Such a *contractionary fiscal policy* should lower the level of aggregate demand, and the economy will experience less employment, a lower price level or both.

From *Master Curriculum Guide in Economics: Teaching Strategies for High School Economics Courses* (New York: National Council on Economic Education, 1985), pp. 151-152

Part A

Decide whether each of the following fiscal policies of the federal government is expansionary or contractionary. Write *expansionary* or *contractionary*, and explain the reasons for your choice.

1. The government cuts business and personal income taxes and increases its own spending.

2. The government increases the personal income tax, Social Security tax and corporate income tax. Government spending stays the same.

3. Government spending goes up while taxes remain the same.

4. The government reduces the wages of its employees while raising taxes on consumers and businesses. Other government spending remains the same.

Part B
Effects of Fiscal Policy

Test your understanding of fiscal policy by completing the table in Figure 30.1. Your choices for each situation must be consistent — that is, you should choose either an expansionary or contractionary fiscal policy. (Fiscal policy cannot provide a solution to one of the situations.) Fill in the spaces as follows:

Column A: Objective for Aggregate Demand
    Draw an up arrow if you wish to increase aggregate demand.
    Draw a down arrow if you wish to decrease aggregate demand.

Column B: Action on Taxes
    Draw an up arrow if you wish to increase taxes.
    Draw a down arrow if you wish to decrease taxes.

Column C: Action on Government Spending
    Draw an up arrow if you wish to increase government spending.
    Draw a down arrow if you wish to decrease government spending.

Column D: Effect on Federal Budget
    Write *toward deficit* if your action will increase the deficit (or reduce the surplus).
    Write *toward surplus* if your action will reduce the deficit (or increase the surplus).

Column E: Effect on the National Debt
    Draw an up arrow if you think the national debt will increase.
    Draw a down arrow if you think the national debt will decrease.

 Figure 30.1
Effects of Fiscal Policy

	(A) Objective for Aggregate Demand	(B) Action on Taxes	(C) Action on Government Spending	(D) Effect on Federal Budget	(E) Effect on the National Debt
1. National unemployment rate rises to 12 percent.	↑	↓	↑	DEFICIT	↑
2. Inflation is strong at a rate of 14 percent per year.	↓	↑	↓	SURPLUS	↓
3. Surveys show consumers are losing confidence in the economy, retail sales are weak and business inventories are increasing rapidly.	↑	↓	↑	DEFICIT	↑
4. Business sales and investment are expanding rapidly, and economists think strong inflation lies ahead.	↓	↑	↓	SURPLUS	↓
5. Inflation persists while unemployment stays high. (stagflation)					

contractionary: AD is too high.
↓ gov't spending
↑ taxes

Discretionary and Automatic Fiscal Policy

One of the goals of economic policy is to stabilize the economy. This means trying to keep employment high and the price level stable. To accomplish this, the amount of aggregate demand in the economy must be near the full-employment level of output. If aggregate demand is too low, there will be unemployment. If aggregate demand is too high, there will be inflation.

Expansionary fiscal policy

contractionary fiscal policy

If aggregate demand is too low, government may be able to stimulate spending in the economy by increasing its spending or by cutting taxes. These policies are examples of *expansionary fiscal policy*. If government wants to slow down aggregate demand, it would pursue a *contractionary fiscal policy*. To do this, it could cut government spending or raise taxes.

Discretionary policy

Automatic Stabilizer

If government has to pass a law or take some other specific action to change its tax and/or spending policies, then government is stabilizing the economy through *discretionary policy*. If the effect happens by itself as the economic situation changes, then it is known as an *automatic stabilizer*. An example of an automatic stabilizer is unemployment compensation: If the economy goes into a recession and people are laid off, they may be eligible to receive unemployment compensation. This payment helps them buy necessities and helps keep aggregate demand from falling as much as it might otherwise. The payments help stabilize the economy but occur without any additional legislation.

As rGDP changes, Fiscal policy automatically changes

Activity written by David Nelson, Western Washington University, Bellingham, Wash.

Listed below are several economic scenarios. For each scenario, indicate whether it represents an automatic (A) or discretionary (D) stabilizer and whether it is an example of expansionary (E) or contractionary (C) fiscal policy. A sample has been completed for you.

Economic Scenarios	Automatic (A) or Discretionary (D)	Expansionary (E) or Contractionary (C)
Sample: Recession raises amount of unemployment compensation.	A	E
1. The government cuts personal income-tax rates.	D	E
2. The government eliminates favorable tax treatment on long-term capital gains.	D	C
3. Incomes rise; as a result, people pay a larger fraction of their income in taxes.	A	C
4. As a result of a recession, more families qualify for food stamps and welfare benefits.	A	E
5. The government eliminates the deductibility of interest expense for tax purposes.	D	C
6. The government launches a major new space program to explore Mars.	D	E
7. The government raises Social Security taxes.	D	C
8. Corporate profits increase; as a result, government collects more corporate income taxes.	A	C
9. The government raises corporate income tax rates.	D	C
10. The government gives all its employees a large pay raise.	D	E

Two Ways to Analyze Fiscal Policy

In Figure 32.1, assume an estimated full-employment national income of $400 billion for the economy and a horizontal SRAS.

✳ Figure 32.1
**Aggregate Expenditure Function
for a Hypothetical Economy**

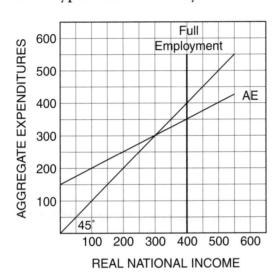

1. What will be the actual national income level in equilibrium? _____

2. Given a marginal propensity to consume of 0.50, how much of an increase in aggregate expenditure would be needed to move the economy to full employment? (Hint: Calculate the MPC from the diagram using the rise divided by the run. Then calculate the multiplier that will operate on any change in AE.) _____

3. How much will GDP increase if aggregate expenditure increases by $50 billion? Why?

4. What fiscal policy measures are available to deal with this situation?

5. Draw in a new AE curve showing the elimination of the gap between the current equilibrium income and the full-employment level of income through the use of fiscal policy. Explain completely the policy you employed.

Adapted from Dascomb R. Forbush and Fredric G. Menz, *Study Guide and Problems to Accompany Lipsey, Steiner and Purvis, Economics,* 8th ed. (New York: HarperCollins Publishing Co., 1987), p. 369.

✳ Figure 32.2
Diagram of a Persistent Gap

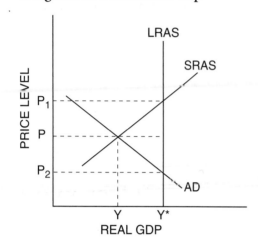

6. Assume a persistent gap between current equilibrium income, Y, and full-employment income, Y*, as shown in Figure 32.2.

   (A) If the government decided not to implement any fiscal policy, the unemployment of resources would eventually lead to a decrease in factor prices. Show diagrammatically that this could eliminate the gap. Label the new curve SRAS$_1$. The new price level would be _____ .

   (B) A second possibility would be to depend on a smaller shift of aggregate supply and have a modest shift in aggregate demand by a discretionary fiscal stimulus so that the price level was maintained at P. Show these two changes in the graph. Label the curves SRAS$_2$ and AD$_1$.

   (C) A third possibility is that government would seek changes in taxes and/or expenditures that would rapidly bring the economy to full employment. Show this diagrammatically. Label the curve AD$_2$.

7. Assume that a hypothetical economy is currently at an equilibrium national income level of $1 trillion, but the full-employment national income is $1.2 trillion. Assume the government's budget is currently in balance at $200 billion and the marginal propensity to consume is 0.75. Fill in the answer blanks or underline the correct words in parentheses.

   (A) The gap between the equilibrium income and full employment is _____ .

   (B) The value of the multiplier is _____ .

   (C) Aggregate expenditures would have to be *(increased / decreased)* by _____ billion to eliminate the gap.

   (D) The government could attempt to eliminate the gap by holding taxes constant and *(increasing / decreasing)* expenditures by _____ billion.

   (E) Alternatively, the government could attempt to eliminate the gap by holding expenditures constant and *(increasing / decreasing)* its tax receipts by _____ billion.

Analyzing the Macroeconomy

Answer the following questions. In some cases, you may also want to include a graph to show your analysis.

1. True, false or uncertain, and explain why? "Regardless of our current economic situation, an increase in aggregate demand will always create new jobs."

2. True, false or uncertain, and explain why? "In the long run, when nominal wages increase, everyone has more money to spend; therefore, the economy as a whole benefits."

3. True, false or uncertain, and explain why? "When unemployment rises, the price level falls. When unemployment falls, the price level rises. It is impossible to have a rising price level with rising unemployment."

4. True, false or uncertain, and explain why? "Our economy is able to adjust to a long-run equilibrium after a decrease in aggregate demand because prices and wages are sticky."

5. True, false or uncertain, and explain why? "If we are in a recession, as long as we continue to increase aggregate demand, we can achieve full employment without driving up the inflation rate."

Activity written by James Stanley, Choate Rosemary Hall, Wallingford, Conn., and John Morton, National Council on Economic Education, New York, N.Y.

6. True, false or uncertain, and explain why? "When the economy experiences an increase in aggregate demand, it will discover that its production possibilities curve has shifted outward."

7. Use short-run AD and AS analysis to illustrate the results of the following events. Then explain why these changes have taken place. Each answer should be accompanied by a clearly labeled diagram.

(A) There is a 25 percent decrease in the price of crude oil.

(B) Price levels in Germany, Japan and Great Britain rise considerably, while price levels in the United States remain unchanged.

(C) The federal government launches a major new highway-construction program.

(D) An insidious computer virus causes all IBM computers in the United States to crash.

(E) There is an increase in worker productivity.

8. Illustrate the following fiscal policy using both the AD and AS model and the Keynesian aggregate expenditure model. In other words, draw two graphs for the fiscal policy change and give a brief explanation of each graph. In your explanation, be sure to emphasize the line of reasoning that generated your results; it is not enough to list the results of your analysis.

Fiscal Policy: At less than full employment, the federal government decreases taxes while holding government spending constant.

Sample Multiple-Choice Questions

Circle the letter of each correct answer.

1. Which of the following best describes aggregate supply?
   (A) The amount buyers plan to spend on output
   (B) A schedule showing the relationship between inputs and outputs
   (C) A schedule showing the trade-off between inflation and unemployment
   (D) A schedule indicating the level of real output that will be purchased at each possible price level
   (E) A schedule indicating the level of real output that will be produced at each possible price level

2. A change in which of the following will cause the aggregate demand curve to shift?
   (A) Energy prices
   (B) Productivity rates
   (C) Consumer wealth
   (D) Prices of inputs
   (E) Prices of consumer goods

3. The short-run aggregate supply curve will shift to the right when
   (A) energy prices increase.
   (B) government regulation increases.
   (C) prices of inputs decrease.
   (D) investment spending decreases.
   (E) productivity rates decrease.

4. A rightward shift in the aggregate demand curve with a horizontal aggregate supply curve will cause employment and the price level to change in which of the following ways?

	Employment	Price Level
(A)	Increase	Increase
(B)	Increase	Decrease
(C)	Increase	No change
(D)	Decrease	No change
(E)	No change	No change

5. An increase in the capital stock will cause the
   (A) aggregate demand curve to shift leftward.
   (B) production possibilities curve to shift in.
   (C) Phillips curve to shift out.
   (D) long-run aggregate supply curve to shift rightward.
   (E) consumption function to shift down.

6. Which of the following is a fiscal policy that would increase aggregate demand in the Keynesian model?
   (A) A decrease in personal income taxes
   (B) A decrease in government spending
   (C) An increase in corporate income taxes
   (D) A purchase of government bonds by the Federal Reserve
   (E) A sale of government bonds by the Federal Reserve

7. An increase in labor productivity would most likely cause real gross domestic product and the price level to change in which of the following ways?

	Real GDP	Price Level
(A)	Increase	Increase
(B)	Increase	Decrease
(C)	Increase	No change
(D)	Decrease	Increase
(E)	Decrease	No change

8. If Maria Escalera's disposable income increases from $600 to $650 and her level of personal-consumption expenditures increase from $480 to $520, you may conclude that her marginal propensity to

(A) consume is 0.8.

(B) consume is 0.4.

(C) consume is 0.25.

(D) save is 0.8.

(E) save is 0.25.

9. In the Keynesian aggregate-expenditure model, if the MPC is 0.75 and gross investment increases by $6 billion, equilibrium GDP will increase by

(A) $6 billion.

(B) $8 billion.

(C) $12 billion.

(D) $24 billion.

(E) $42 billion.

10. In the Keynesian aggregate-expenditure model, the simple spending multiplier can be calculated by dividing

(A) the initial change in spending by the change in real gross domestic product (GDP).

(B) the change in real gross domestic product by the initial change in spending.

(C) one by one minus the marginal propensity to save.

(D) one by one plus the marginal propensity to consume.

(E) the propensity to save by the propensity to consume.

11. Which of the following will cause the consumption schedule to shift upward?

(A) An increase in the amount of consumer indebtedness

(B) A reduction in the wealth or assets held by consumers

(C) An expectation of future declines in the consumer price index

(D) An expectation of future shortages of essential consumer goods

(E) A growing belief that personal income will decline in the future

12. The investment demand curve will shift to the right as the result of

(A) excess productive capacity.

(B) an increase in corporate business taxes.

(C) businesses becoming more optimistic with respect to future business conditions.

(D) recessions in foreign nations that trade with the United States, causing a lower demand for U.S. products.

(E) a decrease in the real interest rate.

13. Automatic stabilizers in the economy include which of the following?

I.   A progressive personal income tax

II. Unemployment compensation

III. Congressional action that increases tax rates

(A) I only

(B) II only

(C) III only

(D) I and II only

(E) I and III only

14. In order to be called an automatic, or built-in, stabilizer, which of the following must taxes automatically do in a recessionary period and in an inflationary period?

	Recessionary Period	Inflationary Period
(A)	Decrease	Decrease
(B)	Decrease	Increase
(C)	Increase	Decrease
(D)	Increase	Increase
(E)	No change	No change

15. The balanced-budget multiplier indicates that

(A) equal increases in government spending and taxation will make a recession worse.

(B) equal increases in government spending and taxation will increase total spending.

(C) government deficits might have a contractionary impact on the economy.

(D) supply will necessarily create its own demand.

(E) the level of gross domestic product is never less than the level of disposable income.

16. In which of the following ways will increases in short-run aggregate supply change the price level and unemployment?

	Price Level	Unemployment
(A)	Increase	No change
(B)	Decrease	Decrease
(C)	Decrease	Increase
(D)	Decrease	No change
(E)	No change	Increase

17. Assume the aggregate supply curve is upward sloping and the economy is in a recession. If the government increases both taxes and government spending by $25 billion, the price level and real GDP will most likely change in which of the following ways?

	Price Level	Real GDP
(A)	Increase	Increase
(B)	Increase	Decrease
(C)	Increase	No Change
(D)	Decrease	Decrease
(E)	Decrease	No Change

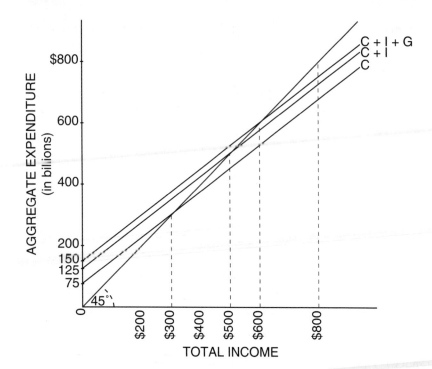

Use the information in the graph above to answer questions 18, 19 and 20. Assume a closed economy with no tax function.

18. Which of the following are true statements about total income?
    I. Equilibrium total income is $800 billion.
    II. Planned investment is $50 billion.
    III. Equilibrium aggregate expenditure is $600 billion.

    (A) I only

    (B) II only

    (C) III only

    (D) I and III only

    (E) II and III only

19. In the graph, if full-employment GDP is $800 billion, the minimum increase in autonomous expenditures that would be required to move total income to full employment income is

    (A) $200 billion.

    (B) $100 billion.

    (C) $50 billion.

    (D) $25 billion.

    (E) zero because total income is already at full employment.

20. In the graph, the values of the MPC, MPS and simple-expenditure multiplier are

	MPC	MPS	Multiplier
(A)	0.5	0.5	2.0
(B)	0.6	0.4	2.5
(C)	0.75	0.25	4.0
(D)	0.8	0.2	5.0
(E)	0.9	0.1	10.0

21. Which of the following fiscal policy actions would be most effective in combating a recession?

	Taxes	Government Spending
(A)	$25 billion decrease	$25 billion decrease
(B)	$25 billion decrease	$25 billion increase
(C)	$25 billion decrease	No change
(D)	$25 billion increase	$25 billion decrease
(E)	$25 billion increase	$25 billion increase

22. If the primary goal is to reduce inflation, which of the following fiscal policy actions would be appropriate during a period of a rapidly increasing consumer price index?

I. Reduce government expenditures for defense and space research.

II. Increase transfer payments to those most severely affected by the rising price index.

III. Increase personal income tax rates.

(A) I only

(B) II only

(C) III only

(D) I and III only

(E) II and III only

23. As the average price level decreases, the purchasing power of people's cash balances increases. This results in an increase in spending. This effect is called

(A) the Laffer effect.

(B) the Keynesian effect.

(C) the money illusion effect.

(D) the real-balance effect.

(E) the neutrality of money.

24. A severe, sustained increase in oil prices would most likely cause short-run and long-run aggregate supply curves and the production possibilities curve to change in which of the following ways?

	Short-Run Aggregate Supply Curve	Long-Run Aggregate Supply Curve	Production Possibilities Curve
(A)	Decrease	No change	Shift outward
(B)	Decrease	Decrease	Shift outward
(C)	Decrease	Decrease	Shift inward
(D)	Increase	No change	No change
(E)	Increase	Increase	Shift inward

25. A decrease in lump-sum personal income taxes will most likely result in an increase in real GDP because which of the following occurs?

I. Government spending decreases to maintain a balanced budget.

II. Consumption spending increases because disposable personal income increases.

III. Investment spending decreases because disposable personal income increases.

(A) I only

(B) II only

(C) III only

(D) I and III only

(E) I, II and III

26. A rapid increase in successful research and development projects for the nation will most likely result in which of the following changes in the short-run and the long-run aggregate supply curves and the production possibilities curve?

	Short-Run Aggregate Supply Curve	Long-Run Aggregate Supply Curve	Production Possibilities Curve
(A)	Decrease	No change	No change
(B)	Decrease	Decrease	Shift inward
(C)	Increase	No change	Shift inward
(D)	Increase	Increase	No change
(E)	Increase	Increase	Shift outward

27. If the marginal propensity to consume is two-thirds, then an increase in personal income taxes of $100 will most likely result in

(A) a decrease in consumption of $100.

(B) a decrease in autonomous investment of $100.

(C) a decrease in consumption of $67 and an increase in savings of $33.

(D) a decrease in consumption of $67 and a decrease in savings of $33.

(E) an increase in government spending of more than $100.

28. An increase in personal income taxes will most likely result in which of the following changes in real GDP and the price level in the short-run?

	Real GDP	Price Level
(A)	Decrease	Decrease
(B)	Decrease	Increase
(C)	Increase	No change
(D)	Increase	Increase
(E)	Increase	No change

29. One of the reasons the aggregate demand curve is downward sloping is that as the value of cash balances decreases, aggregate spending decreases. This is called

(A) a positive externality.

(B) a negative spillover.

(C) the Pareto effect.

(D) the substitution effect.

(E) the real-balance effect.

30. If there is a decrease in the short-run aggregate supply curve and no changes in monetary and fiscal policies are implemented, the economy over time will

(A) remain at the new price and output level.

(B) continue to have rising prices and decreasing real GDP.

(C) experience increasing nominal wages.

(D) return to the original output and price level.

(E) experience a leftward shift in the aggregate demand curve.

Sample Short Free-Response Questions

1. In the 1960s many newspaper reporters were accustomed to reporting a decrease in the unemployment rate when the overall price level increased. However, in the 1970s, when increases in the overall price level were accompanied by increases, not decreases, in the unemployment rate, some reporters went so far as to declare macroeconomics "bankrupt" and unable to explain this "mystery."

   Using short-run aggregate demand and aggregate supply analysis, explain the "mystery" of why the increases in the overall price level during the 1960s might have been accompanied by decreases in the unemployment rate and the increases in the overall price level during the 1970s might have been accompanied by increases in the unemployment rate.

2. The U.S. stock market declined dramatically from 2000 to 2003.

   (A) What did this decline mean?

   (B) What were the possible effects of this decline on the U.S. economy's output, prices and employment?

3. Some economists claim that investment spending is more important than consumption spending in causing changes in the business cycle. However, investment spending is only one-fourth of consumption spending. Explain why investment spending can be so important if it is so much less than consumption spending.

4. In 1981, factories used 79 percent of their capacity. In 1982, factories used 71 percent of their capacity. In which year do you think the economy was on a steeper portion of its short-run aggregate supply curve? Explain.

5. Recently, an economist was asked if the Great Depression could occur again. The reply was, "It is possible, but we have many more automatic stabilizers today than we had in 1929." Describe three automatic stabilizers and explain how they might prevent a depression.

6. A town's largest industry invests $50 million to expand its plant capacity. Without using a formula, explain how this expenditure will affect the town's economy through the multiplier effect.

7. Throughout most of the decade of the 1990s, gains were made in productivity. What effect do these yearly gains have on the short-run aggregate supply curve? Is there any change in long-run aggregate supply?

Sample Long Free-Response Questions

1. Assume you are a member of Congress. A member of your staff has just given you the following economic statistics:

	Year Ago Quarter	Last Quarter	Estimate for Quarter Now Ending
Real gross domestic product (in billions of 1997 dollars)	$2,789	$2,689	$2,598
Consumer price index	197	201	204
Unemployment rate	5%	8%	10.2%
Gross private investment (in billions of 1997 dollars)	$312	$300	$287

(A) What economic problem is this nation facing?

(B) Identify the fiscal policy actions you would recommend.

(C) What are the goals of your fiscal policy actions?

(D) Explain how each policy action you identified in Question 1(B) will fit the goals you stated in Question 1(C).

(E) Use a correctly labeled aggregate demand and aggregate supply graph to show the effects of your fiscal policy on the economy. Show the changes that will occur in the price level and the level of real GDP.

2. Assume you are a member of Congress. A staff member has just given you the following economic statistics:

	Year Ago Quarter	Last Quarter	Estimate for Quarter Now Ending
Real gross domestic product (in billions of 1997 dollars)	$2,356	$2,589	$2,752
Consumer price index	210	240	250
Unemployment rate	10%	6.5%	5.1%
Gross private investment (in billions of 1997 dollars)	$312	$340	$352

(A) What economic problem is this nation facing?

(B) Identify the fiscal policy actions you would recommend.

(C) What are the goals of your fiscal policy actions?

(D) Explain how each policy action you identified in Question 2(B) will fit the goals you stated in Question 2(C).

(E) Use a correctly labeled aggregate demand and aggregate supply graph to show the effects of your fiscal policy on the economy. Show the changes that will occur in the price level and the level of real GDP.

3. Assume that the economy has been operating at the full-employment levels of output and employment but has recently experienced a decrease in consumption spending because of a sharp decline in stock market indexes that has reduced the wealth of the nation by about 18 percent. Consumption expenditures have decreased at all levels of income.

(A) Use correctly labeled aggregate demand and aggregate supply graphs to illustrate the short-run effect of the decrease in consumption expenditures on each of the following:

   (i)   Output

   (ii) Employment

   (iii) The price level

(B) Identify two fiscal policy actions that could be used to counter the effects of the initial decrease in consumption spending. Explain, using correctly labeled aggregate demand and aggregate supply graphs, the short-run effects of each of your policies on each of the following:

(i) Output

(ii) Employment

(iii) The price level

4. Assume that political problems restrict the supply of oil in international markets. Consequently, increased production costs result in the following economic conditions in the United States:

■ The unemployment rate is 8 percent and rising.

■ The CPI is rising 9 percent annually and accelerating.

■ The annual rate of growth of real GDP is −1.5 percent.

(A) Identify and describe the major macroeconomic problems in the economy. Using correctly labeled aggregate demand and aggregate supply graphs, show the condition of the economy.

(B) With a federal budget deficit of nearly $350 billion, fiscal authorities are considering the following policy actions to address the existing economic problems:

Policy 1: Increase government expenditures.

Policy 2: Increase personal income taxes.

Policy 3: Decrease business taxes and regulations.

Describe the effect of each of the policies on the economy, and demonstrate each on an individual aggregate demand and aggregate supply graph. Be sure to include each of the following in your description:

(i) Output

(ii) Employment

(iii) The price level

Policy 1:

Policy 2:

Policy 3:

Macroeconomics | Unit 4

Money, Monetary Policy and Economic Stability

- Throughout history, there have been four basic types of money: commodity money, representative money, fiat money and check-book money.

- Money has three main functions: a medium of exchange, a standard of value (or unit of account) and a store of value.

- To accomplish its functions, the characteristics of money include portability, uniformity, acceptability, durability, divisibility and stability in value.

- M1 is the narrowest definition of money and consists of checkable deposits, traveler's checks and currency. Checkable deposits include demand deposits and account for about 75 percent of M1.

- M2 and M3 are broader definitions of money and include savings accounts and other time deposits.

- The demand for money is the sum of transactions demand, precautionary demand and speculative demand. The demand for money is determined by interest rates, income and the price level.

- MV = PQ is the equation of exchange: Money times velocity equals price times quantity of goods. PQ is the nominal GDP.

- Velocity is the number of times a year that the money supply is used to make payments for final goods and services:

$$V = \frac{GDP}{M}$$

- Money is created when banks make loans. One bank's loan becomes another bank's demand deposit. Demand deposits are money. When a loan is repaid, money is destroyed.

- Banks are required to keep a percentage of their deposits as reserves. Reserves can be currency in the bank vault or deposits at the Federal Reserve Banks. This reserve requirement limits the amount of money banks can create.

- The simple deposit expansion multiplier is equal to 1 divided by the required reserve ratio (rr).

$$\text{Deposit expansion multiplier} = \frac{1}{rr}$$

- The higher the reserve requirement, the less money can be created; the lower the reserve requirement, the more money can be created.

- The Federal Reserve regulates financial institutions and controls the nation's money supply. The three main tools that the Fed uses to control the money supply are buying and selling government bonds on the open market (open market operations), changing the discount rate and changing the reserve requirement.

- If the Fed wants to encourage bank lending and increase the money supply, it will buy bonds on the open market, decrease the discount rate or decrease the reserve requirement. This is referred to as expansionary monetary policy or an easy money policy and is used by the Fed to reduce unemployment.

- If the Fed wants to hold down or decrease the money supply, it will discourage bank lending by selling bonds on the open market, increasing the discount rate or increasing the reserve requirement. This is called a contractionary monetary policy or a tight money policy and is used by the Fed to discourage bank lending during periods of inflation.

- Open market operations are the most frequently used tool because they permit the Fed to make small changes in the money supply and can be implemented immediately.

- Changes in the reserve requirement can have substantial economic effects, and thus the Fed rarely changes the reserve requirement. The Fed uses changes in the discount rate primarily as a signal of a change in the direction of monetary policy.

- The Fed cannot target both the money supply and interest rates simultaneously, so it must choose which variable to target.

- The Fed currently targets the federal funds rate rather than the money supply to implement monetary policy. It targets the federal funds rate because the Fed believes that this rate is closely tied to economic activity.

- The federal funds rate is the interest rate a bank charges when it lends excess reserves to other banks.

Money

Throughout history, a wide variety of items have served as money. These include gold, silver, large stone wheels, tobacco, beer, dog teeth, porpoise teeth, cattle, metal coins, paper bills and checks. All of these types of money should be judged on how well they accomplish the functions of money. Money is what money does!

The functions of money are to serve as a medium of exchange, a standard of value and a store of value.

To be a good *medium of exchange*, money must be *accepted by people* when they buy and sell goods and services. It should be *portable* or easily carried from place to place. It must also be *divisible* so that large and small transactions can be made. It must also be *uniform* so that a particular unit such as a quarter represents the same value as every other quarter.

To be a good *standard of value*, or *unit of account*, money must be useful for quoting prices. To accomplish this, money must be *familiar, divisible* and *accepted.*

To be a good *store of value*, money must be *durable* so it can be kept for future use. It also should have a *stable value* so people do not lose purchasing power if they use the money at a later time.

Money is any item or commodity that is generally accepted in payment for goods and services or in repayment of debts, and serves as an asset to its holder.

Activity written by John Morton, National Council on Economic Education, New York, N.Y., and revised by Charles A. Bennett, Gannon University, Erie, Pa.

1. Use the table below to evaluate how well each item would perform the functions of money in today's economy. If an item seems to fulfill the function, put a **+** sign in the box; if it does not fulfill a function in your opinion, place a **–** sign in the box. Put a **?** sign in the box if you are unsure whether the item fulfills the functions of money. The item with the most **+** signs would be the best form of money for you. In the space below the table, list the top six forms of money, according to your evaluation.

Item	Medium of Exchange	Store of Value	Standard of Value
Salt	+	–	–
Large stone wheels	–	–	–
Cattle	–	–	+
Gold	+	–	+
Copper coins	+	–	+
Beaver pelts	–	–	–
Personal checks	+	+	+
Savings account passbook	+	+	+
Prepaid phone card	+	–	+
Debit card	+	+	+
Credit card	+	+	+
Cigarettes	+	–	+
Playing cards	+	–	–
Bushels of wheat	+	–	+
$1 bill	+	+	+
$100 bill	+	+	+

Your top six forms of money:

personal checks

savings account passbook

debit card

credit card

$1 bill

$100 bill

2. After you finish the evaluation in Question 1, rate the various items in the table below. Evaluate how well they meet the characteristics of money. Again, if an item seems to fit a characteristic, use a **+** sign; if the item does not seem to fit a characteristic, use a **−** sign. If there is a difference of opinion or if you are uncertain, use a **?** sign. The item with the most **+** signs would best fit the characteristics of money. In the space below the table, list your six top items.

Item	Portability	Uniformity	Acceptability	Durability	Stability in Value
Salt	+	−	−	−	+
Large stone wheels	−	−	−	−	−
Cattle	−	−	−	−	+
Gold	+	−	−	−	+
Copper coins	+	−	−	−	−
Beaver pelts	+				
Personal checks	+	+	+		
Savings account passbook	+	+	+	+	+
Prepaid phone card	+	−	−	−	−
Debit card	+	+	+	+	+
Credit card	+	+	+	+	+
Cigarettes					
Playing cards					
Bushels of wheat					
$1 bill					
$100 bill					

Your top six items: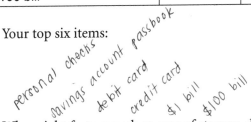
personal checks
savings account passbook
debit card
credit card
$1 bill
$100 bill

3. Why might factors such as ease of storage, difficulty in counterfeiting and security of electronic transfer of funds also be characteristics that you might use in evaluating money?

What's All This About the Ms?

While monetary policy is the subject of debates that capture the public's attention, the first steps in the formulation of policy may appear relatively mundane. We must first define and measure the money supply. Defining and measuring money has become an increasingly difficult task because of reforms in the financial system, and because people and banks hold money in myriad different forms.

Money Defined...

There is general agreement on a simple conceptual *definition* of money. However, the complexity of the real world and our rapidly evolving financial system prevent agreement on a single *measure* of money, and this can cause confusion.

The Federal Reserve defines monetary aggregates by grouping assets that the public uses in roughly similar ways. In defining these measures of money, the Fed draws somewhat arbitrary lines between groups of assets that serve in varying degrees as both the medium-of-exchange and store-of-value functions of money.

Depository institutions such as banks, savings and loan associations and credit unions report to the Fed the value of their time and savings deposits, vault cash and transaction accounts such as checkable deposits.

The data on checkable deposits are the primary source for the calculation of required reserves and the construction of the monetary aggregates. The Fed's Board of Governors and the Federal Open Market Committee use this information in the formulation of monetary policy.

... and Measured

M1 is the narrowest definition and measure of the money supply. It includes assets used primarily for transactions or as a medium of exchange. M1 includes currency and coin held by the nonbank public, demand deposits, other checkable deposits and traveler's checks.

M2 is a broader measure of money stock. In addition to the items included in M1, M2 includes the amount held in savings and small time deposits, money market deposit accounts (MMDAs), noninstitutional money market mutual funds (MMMFs) and certain other short-term money market assets.

M3 is an even broader definition of the money supply. It includes all of the components of M2 plus a number of financial assets and instruments generally employed by large businesses and financial institutions.

We can look at the three definitions of money in the following terms:

■ M1 includes items that are primarily used as a medium of exchange.

■ M2 includes items that are used as a store of value.

■ M3 includes items that serve as a unit of account.

Activity from *Econ Ed* (New York: The Federal Reserve Bank of New York, September 1987) and revised by Robert Wedge, Massachusetts Council on Economic Education, Waltham, Mass.

The Fed considers a number of factors when it measures the monetary aggregates, but ultimately what matters is how the public uses the different forms of money available. For example, depositors can write checks on their MMDAs or their MMMFs. The public, however, primarily uses these types of accounts for savings and only secondarily for transactions. Therefore, these accounts are typically placed in M2 with savings accounts and time deposits, which also primarily serve the store-of-value function of money.

On the other hand, deposits in NOW (negotiable order of withdrawal) accounts are included in M1 because they are primarily used as a medium of exchange, even though they earn interest and depositors use them for savings.

1. What are the three basic functions of money?

2. Why is it important for the Fed to know the size and rate of growth of the money supply?

    (A) What are the effects if the money supply grows too slowly?

    (B) What are the effects if the money supply grows too rapidly?

3. Name a type of money that serves primarily as a medium of exchange.

4. Name a type of money that serves primarily as a store of value.

5. With the use of credit cards becoming more prominent and the availability of credit broader than ever, why are credit cards not included in the Ms?

Advanced Placement Economics Macroeconomics: Student Activities © Council For Economic Education, New York, N.Y.

6. Why is it difficult for the Fed to get an accurate measure of the money supply?

7. Why must the Fed continue to develop new ways to track the money supply?

8. Use the data in Figure 35.1 to calculate M1, M2 and M3. Assume that all items not mentioned are zero. Show all components for your answers.

Figure 35.1
Calculating the Ms

Checkable deposits (demand deposits, NOW, ATM and credit union share draft accounts)	$850
Currency	$200
Large time deposits	$800
Noncheckable savings deposits	$302
Small time deposits	$1,745
Institutional money market mutual funds	$1,210

M1 = _____

M2 = ___3,097_____

don't count in M1 ↣M2

M3 = _____

The Monetary Equation of Exchange

Economists use an equation made famous by Irving Fisher to show the relationship among money, price and real output. This equation is called the *equation of exchange*, and it typically takes the following form:

MV = PQ

M = the amount of money in circulation

V = the income velocity of money → *spending becomes income for other people*

P = the average price level

Q = real GDP or real value of all final goods and services

    This equation attempts to show the balance between "money," which is represented on the left side of the equation, and goods and services, which are represented on the right side. For a given level of income velocity, if the supply of money grows faster than the rate of real output (changes in Q), then there will be inflation in the economy. Classical economists assumed that the velocity of money was stable (constant) over time because institutional factors — such as how frequently people are paid — largely determine velocity.

$$M\underline{V} = PQ \rightarrow \frac{GDP \uparrow}{MKT\ BSKT\ PL}$$

Activity written by Robert Wedge, Massachusetts Council on Economic Education, Waltham, Mass.

Part A

1. Define (in your own words and in one or two sentences each) the four variables in the equation of exchange.

   The M is money essentially in circulation (checks, cash, etc.)
   The V is spending becomes income for other people.
   The p is average price level.
   The Q is the rGDP.

2. The product of velocity (V) and the money supply (M) equals PQ. How can PQ be defined?

   "it depends"
   roughly nominal GDP

3. Suppose velocity remains constant, while the money supply increases. Explain how this would affect nominal GDP.

   It depends

4. During the past 30 years, the use of credit cards has increased, and banks and financial institutions increasingly use computers for transactions. Explain how these changes might affect velocity.

   Spend the money more quickly; instead of having to visit physical banks and such.
   Velocity of money is increased.

5. As the result of legislative and regulatory reform throughout the 1980s and 1990s, banks and other financial institutions began paying interest on a significant proportion of the checkable deposits in the M1 definition of the money supply. Explain how these changes might be expected to affect the velocity of M1.

   If money is earning interest rates, people
   are less likely to spend what they have in their
   checking accounts.

Part B

The following tables give data on money supply, prices, real GDP and velocity for the U.S. economy for 14 recent years. Because of rounding, some totals may not come out exactly.

6. Complete the tables by filling in the blanks.

 Figure 36.1
M1 Chart

Year	M1 (billions of $)	V	P Implicit Price Deflator for GDP	Q Real GDP (billions of $)	PQ Nominal GDP (billions of $)
1987	$750	6.36	0.780	$6,114	$4,768.90
1988	786	6.48	0.800	6,370	5,096.00
1989	792	6.93	0.833	6,592	5,489.00
1990	824	7.00	0.860	6,707	5,768.00
1991	896	6.71	0.90	6,677	6,009.30
1992	1,024	6.18	0.920	6,880	6,329.60
1993	1,129	5.88	0.940	7,063	6,639.20
1994	1,150	6.13	0.960	7,343	7,054.30
1995	1,125	6.57	0.980	7,544	7,393.10
1996	1,080	7.23	1.000	7,813	7,813.00
1997	1,073	7.76	1.020	8,160	8,323.20
1998	1,097	7.99	1.030	8,510	8,765.30
1999	1,125	8.28	1.050	8,876	9,319.80
2000	1,088	8.98	1.0691	9,320	9,768.90

 Figure 36.2
M2 Chart

Year	M2 (billions of $; Dec. figures)	V	P Implicit Price Deflator for GDP	Q Real GDP (billions of $)	PQ Nominal GDP (billions of $)
1987	$2,830	1.68	0.78	$6,114	$4,769
1988	2,994	1.70	0.80	6,370	5,096
1989	3,158	1.74	0.83	6,592	5,489
1990	3,277	1.76	0.86	6,707	5,768
1991	3,377	1.78	0.90	6,677	6,009
1992	3,431	1.84	0.92	6,880	6,330
1993	3,484	1.91	0.94	7,063	6,639
1994	3,500	2.02	0.96	7,348	7,054
1995	3,642	2.03	0.98	7,544	7,393
1996	3,815	2.05	1.00	7,813	7,813
1997	4,032	2.06	1.02	8,143	8,318
1998	4,395	2.00	1.03	8,510	8,790
1999	4,653	2.00	1.05	8,876	9,299
2000	4,945	2.01	1.07	9,319	9,963

7. What might one infer from the changes of the 1980s and 1990s about the classical assumption that institutional factors determine velocity?

8. Use the grid below and the M1 and M2 data to graph the income velocity from 1987 to 2000.

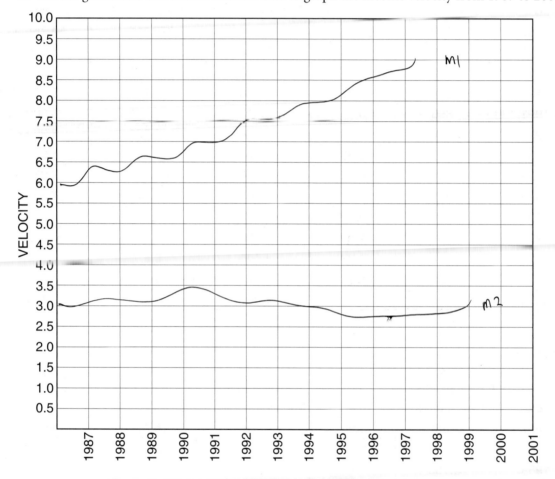

(A) What trends do you see?

(B) What is the difference in the value of M1 velocity and M2 velocity? Explain why they are different.

9. For a given money supply growth, a(n) (*increase / decrease*) in velocity will (*increase / decrease*) inflationary pressure. (Underline the correct word(s) in parentheses.)

The Multiple Expansion of Checkable Deposits

This activity is designed to illustrate how banks' lending of excess reserves can expand the nation's money supply and to explain how the Federal Reserve System can limit the growth of the money supply using the required reserve ratio.

Part A

Assume that

- the required reserve ratio is 10 percent of checkable deposits and banks lend out the other 90 percent of their deposits (banks wish to hold no excess reserves) and
- all money lent out by one bank is redeposited in another bank.

1. Under these assumptions, if a new checkable deposit of $1,000 is made in Bank 1,

    (A) how much will Bank 1 keep as required reserves? $_____

    (B) how much will Bank 1 lend out? $_____

    (C) how much will be redeposited in Bank 2? $_____

    (D) how much will Bank 2 keep as required reserves? $_____

    (E) how much will Bank 2 lend out? $_____

    (F) how much will be redeposited in Bank 3? $_____

2. Use your answers to Question 1 to help you complete the table in Figure 37.1. Fill in the blanks in the table, rounding numbers to the second decimal (for example, $59.049 = $59.05). After you have completed the table, answer the questions that follow by filling in the blanks or underlining the correct answer in parentheses so each statement is true.

 Figure 37.1

Checkable Deposits, Reserves and Loans in Seven Banks

Bank No.	New Checkable Deposits	10% Fractional Reserves	Loans
1	$1,000.00	$100.00	$900.00
2	900.00		810.00
3		81.00	
4			656.10
5			
6		59.05	
7	531.44		478.30
All other banks combined			
Total for all banks	$10,000.00		$9,000.00

3. In this example:

   (A) The original deposit of $1,000 increased total bank reserves by $_____. Eventually, this led to a total of $10,000 expansion of bank deposits, _____ of which was because of the original deposit, while _____ was because of bank lending activities.

   (B) Therefore, if the fractional reserve had been 15 percent instead of 10 percent, the amount of deposit expansion would have been *(more / less)* than in this example.

   (C) Therefore, if the fractional reserve had been 5 percent instead of 10 percent, the amount of deposit expansion would have been *(more / less)* than in this example.

   (D) If banks had not loaned out all of their excess reserves, the amount of deposit expansion would have been *(more / less)* than in this example.

   (E) If all loans had not been redeposited in the banking system, the amount of deposit expansion would have been *(more / less)* than in this example.

4. Another way to represent the multiple expansion of deposits is through *T-accounts*. In short, a T-account is an accounting relationship that looks at changes in balance sheet items. Since balance sheets must balance, so, too, must T-accounts. T-account entries on the asset side must be balanced by an offsetting asset or an offsetting liability. A sample T-account is provided below. For the bank, *assets* include accounts at the Federal Reserve District Bank, Treasury securities and loans; *liabilities* are deposits and *net worth* is assets minus liabilities. Show how the $1,000 checkable deposit described in Question 1 would be listed in a T-account.

Assets	Liabilities

Part B

The Federal Reserve sets the reserve requirements: the percentages of the bank's deposits that the bank must hold as reserves. Banks may not loan out these required reserves. As we said in Part A, this fractional reserve system actually allows banks to create money. The amount of reserves a bank holds is known as its *total reserves*. Total reserves are composed of *required reserves*, which the bank must keep, and *excess reserves*, which the bank can loan to other customers. The reserves held by the bank beyond those required by the Fed are *excess reserves*.

How much money would be created if the bank continued to loan out its excess reserves to the last penny? To find out, we must calculate the *deposit expansion multiplier*. The deposit expansion multiplier determines how much money can be created in the economy from an initial deposit. The formula for the deposit expansion multiplier is

$$\textbf{Deposit expansion multiplier} \; = \; \frac{1}{\textbf{reserve requirement}}$$

In the example in Part A, the Federal Reserve set the reserve requirement at 10 percent. So the deposit expansion multiplier would be

$$\textbf{Deposit expansion multiplier} \; = \frac{1}{0.10} \; = \; 10$$

To find the maximum amount of money that could be created, the formula is

Expansion of the money supply = deposit expansion multiplier x excess reserves

The multiplier is 10, and excess reserves from the initial bank deposit are $900. So the potential expansion of money (M1) would be

Expansion of the money supply = 10 x $900 = $9,000

M1 now consists of the original $1,000 deposit plus the $9,000 created.

---

5. Assume that $1,000 is deposited in the bank, and that each bank loans out all of its excess reserves. For each of the following required reserve ratios, calculate the amount that the bank must hold in required reserves, the amount that will be excess reserves, the deposit expansion multiplier and the maximum amount that the money supply could increase.

	Required Reserve Ratio					
	1%	5%	10%	12.5%	15%	25%
Required reserves						
Excess reserves						
Deposit expansion multiplier						
Maximum increase in the money supply						

6. If the required reserve ratio were 0 percent, then money supply expansion would be infinite. Why don't we want an infinite growth of the money supply? (Hint: remember the equation of exchange: $MV = PQ$.)

7. If the Federal Reserve wants to increase the money supply, should it raise or lower the reserve requirement? Why?

8. If the Federal Reserve increases the reserve requirement and velocity remains stable, what will happen to nominal GDP? Why?

9. What economic goal might the Federal Reserve try to meet by reducing the money supply?

10. Why might the money supply not expand by the amount predicted by the deposit expansion multiplier?

Advanced Placement Economics Macroeconomics: Student Activities © Council For Economic Education, New York, N.Y.

The Federal Reserve: The Mechanics of Monetary Policy

To manage the money supply, the Federal Reserve uses the tools of monetary policy to influence the quantity of reserves in the banking system. Increasing (decreasing) reserves tends to expand (contract) a bank's ability to make loans. Thus, reserve management gives the Fed powerful influence over the money supply and, in turn, over the general price level. The primary tool for reserve management today is open market operations (OMO). Discount rate changes serve primarily as signals; reserve requirements are rarely changed. Using T-accounts, Figures 38.1 and 38.2 show how the Fed could use open market operations to increase the money supply by $100.

Example: Baseline case

Figure 38.1 shows a baseline T-account. The required reserve ratio is 10 percent of checking deposits. With $26 in reserve accounts and $4 in Federal Reserve notes (vault cash), total bank reserves equal $30, exactly 10 percent of checkable deposits (in other words, no excess reserves). Net worth = assets – liabilities.

Figure 38.1
Baseline Case

Assets			Liabilities
	The Fed		
Treasury securities	$83	$26	Reserve accounts of banks
		$57	Federal Reserve notes
	Banks		
Reserve accounts	$26	$300	Checkable deposits
Federal Reserve notes	$4		
Loans	$405	$135	Net worth (to stockholders)
	Bank Customers		
Checkable deposits	$300	$405	Loans
Federal Reserve notes	$53		
Treasury securities	$52		
	Money supply = $353 ($300 + $53)		

Activity written by Robert Graboyes, University of Richmond, Richmond, Va.

Example: Expansionary policy via open market purchases

Suppose the Fed believes the economy is heading into a recession and wishes to increase the money supply by $100. Using open market operations, the Fed purchases $10 worth of Treasury securities from the public.

Figure 38.2 shows the consolidated accounts after the changes of this Fed action work their way through the economy. Changes are shown in boldface. Be sure to compare Figure 38.1 with Figure 38.2 to see the changes. The Fed's $10 increase in reserve accounts yields a $100 increase in the money supply.

Figure 38.2
After $10 Open Market Purchase

Assets			Liabilities
The Fed			
Treasury securities (**+$10**)	**$93**	**$36**	Reserve accounts of banks (**+$10**)
		$57	Federal Reserve notes
Banks			
Reserve accounts (**+$10**)	**$36**	**$400**	Checkable deposits (**+$100**)
Federal Reserve notes	$4		
Loans (**+$90**)	**$495**	$135	Net worth (to stockholders)
Bank Customers			
Checkable deposits (**+$100**)	**$400**	**$495**	Loans (**+$90**)
Federal Reserve notes	$53		
Treasury securities (**– $10**)	**$42**		
Money supply = **$453** (**$400 + $53**)			

For Questions 1 through 4, start with the baseline case in Figure 38.1. The Fed wishes to *decrease* the money supply from $353 to $303 by open market operations. The reserve requirement is 10 percent.

1. Will the Fed want to buy or sell existing Treasury securities? _____

2. What is the money multiplier? _____

3. What is the value of Treasury securities that need to be bought or sold? _____

4. Fill in Figure 38.3 to show the accounts after open market operations are finished and all changes have worked their way through the economy:

Figure 38.3
After Open Market Operations Are Finished

Assets			Liabilities
	The Fed		
Treasury securities	___		Reserve accounts of banks
		$57	Federal Reserve notes
	Banks		
Reserve accounts	___		Checkable deposits
Federal Reserve notes	___		
Loans		$135	Net worth (to stockholders)
	Bank Customers		
Checkable deposits	___		Loans
Federal Reserve notes	$53		
Treasury securities	___		
	Money supply = _____		

For Questions 5 through 7, suppose banks keep zero excess reserves and the reserve requirement is 15 percent.

5. What is the deposit expansion multiplier? _____

6. A customer deposits $100,000 in his checking account.

    (A) How much of this can the bank lend to new customers? _____

    (B) How much must the bank add to its reserves? _____

    (C) In what two forms can a bank hold the new required reserves?

7. Suppose that the $100,000 had previously been held in Federal Reserve notes under the customer's mattress and that banks continue to hold no excess reserves. By how much will the customer's deposit cause the money supply to grow? _____

8. A very low discount rate may (encourage banks to borrow / discourage banks from borrowing) from the Federal Reserve. Underline the correct answer and explain why.

9. The federal funds rate is the interest rate at which financial institutions can borrow from other financial institutions. Suppose the federal funds rate is 5 percent and the discount rate is 4.5 percent. Why is it that a bank might choose to borrow in the federal funds market, rather than getting the lower interest rate available through the discount window?

10. In a foreign country, the reserve requirement is 100 percent. What will be the deposit expansion multiplier? _____

11. If the Fed decided to implement a policy action designed to increase the money supply, in which direction would bank reserves and the federal funds rate change and why?

Advanced Placement Economics Macroeconomics: Student Activities © Council For Economic Education, New York, N.Y.

12. Circle the correct symbol (↑ for increase, ↓ for decrease) in Figure 38.4.

Figure 38.4
Fed Actions and Their Effects

Federal Reserve Action	Bank Reserves	Money Supply	Fed Funds Rate
A. Sold Treasury securities on the open market	↑ ↓	↑ ↓	↑ ↓
B. Bought Treasury securities on the open market	↑ ↓	↑ ↓	↑ ↓
C. Raised the discount rate	↑ ↓	↑ ↓	↑ ↓
D. Lowered the discount rate	↑ ↓	↑ ↓	↑ ↓
E. Raised the reserve requirement	↑ ↓	↑ ↓	↑ ↓
F. Lowered the reserve requirement	↑ ↓	↑ ↓	↑ ↓

13. Indicate in the table in Figure 38.5 how the Federal Reserve could use each of the three monetary policy tools to pursue an expansionary policy and a contractionary policy.

Figure 38.5
Tools of Monetary Policy

Monetary Policy	Expansionary Policy	Contractionary Policy
A. Open market operations		
B. Discount rate		
C. Reserve requirements		

14. Why do banks hold excess reserves, which pay no interest?

15. Why does the Fed rarely use the reserve requirement as an instrument of monetary policy?

16. What does it mean to say that the Fed changes the discount rate mostly as a *signal* to markets?

17. Why does the Fed currently target the federal funds rate rather than the money supply?

The Money Market

The money market consists of the demand for money and the supply of money. We generally assume that the Federal Reserve determines the supply of money. Thus, the supply of money is a vertical line. The demand for money is based on a decision of whether to hold your wealth in the form of interest bearing assets (savings accounts, stocks, etc.) or as money (noninterest bearing). The demand for money is a function of interest rates and income, and is determined by three motives:

■ Transactions demand — the demand for money to make purchases of goods and services

■ Precautionary demand — the demand for money to serve as protection against an unexpected need

■ Speculative demand — the demand for money because it serves as a store of wealth

The interest rate represents the opportunity cost of holding money; that is, the interest rate represents the forgone income you might have made had you held an interest-bearing asset rather than money, a noninterest-bearing asset. Thus the demand for money has an inverse relationship with the interest rate. The demand curve represents the demand for money at various levels of the interest rate for the given income level (GDP). The graph of the money market looks like this:

 Figure 39.1
The Money Market

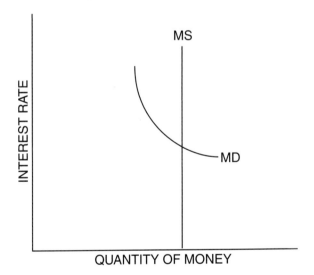

Activity written by Rae Jean B. Goodman, U.S. Naval Academy, Annapolis, Md.

1. Suppose the Federal Reserve increases the money supply by buying Treasury securities.

   (A) What happens to the interest rate?

   (B) What happens to the quantity of money demanded?

   (C) Explain what happens to loans and interest rates as the Fed increases the money supply.

2. Suppose the demand for money increases.

   (A) What happens to the interest rate?

   (B) What happens to the quantity of money supplied?

   (C) If the Fed wants to maintain a constant interest rate when the demand for money increases, explain what policy the Fed needs to follow and why.

   (D) Why might the Fed want to maintain a constant interest rate?

✳ Figure 39.2
Alternative Money Demand Curves

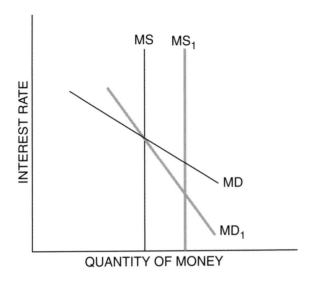

3. Suppose there are two money demand curves — MD and MD₁ — and the Fed increases the money supply from MS to MS₁ as shown in Figure 39.2.

   (A) Compare what happens to the interest rate with each MD curve.

   (B) Explain the effect of the change in the money supply on consumption, investment, real output and prices. Would there be a difference in the effects under the two different money demand curves? If so, explain.

   (C) How would you describe, in economic terms, the difference between the two money demand curves?

   (D) If the Federal Reserve is trying to get the economy out of a recession, which money demand curve would it want to represent the economy? Explain.

The Federal Reserve: Monetary Policy and Macroeconomics

The Basics

■ **Purpose of monetary policy:** "To promote effectively the goals of maximum employment, stable prices and moderate long-term interest rates" (*The Federal Reserve System: Purpose and Functions*, Washington D.C.: Federal Reserve Board of Governors, page 17.)

■ **Primary goal since 1979:** To stabilize prices, which is arguably the strongest contribution the Fed can make toward maximizing long-term real output and moderating long-term interest rates

■ **Reason for this goal:** Over time, it has become evident that monetary policy's long-term influence over prices is strong and predictable, but its influence over real output and real interest rates is mostly short-term and not highly predictable.

Linkages That Motivate Monetary Policy

The following diagram illustrates how monetary policy operates and how it affects prices and quantities (real output).

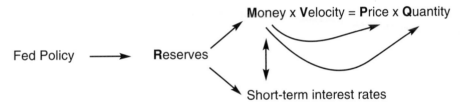

Money x Velocity = Price x Quantity

Fed Policy ⟶ Reserves

Short-term interest rates

The Fed Influences the Money Supply by Managing Reserves

A greater volume of reserves leads banks to expand credit, expanding the money supply through the *money multiplier*.

■ **Tools of policy:** Open market operations are the most frequently used tool. Changes in the discount rate are used primarily to signal the Fed's policy. Reserve requirements are seldom adjusted.

■ **Choice of policy targets:** The Fed can set money supply targets, knowing that such actions will affect short-term interest rates as a by-product. Or the Fed can target short-term interest rates directly. Because of changes in financial institutions and other economic relationships, the optimal operating procedures change over time.

■ **Limitation on policy:** The Fed cannot target the money supply and short-term interest rates simultaneously. *Ceteris paribus*, or all other factors held constant, increasing (decreasing) the money supply decreases (increases) short-term interest rates.

■ **Importance of velocity:** Changes in the money supply have little short-term effect on velocity, so changes in the money supply *must* affect prices or real output, or both. This linkage provides the underlying motive for the long-term conduct of monetary policy.

Activity written by Robert Graboyes, University of Richmond, Richmond, Va.

Economists Can Disagree Sharply Over the Effects of a Given Monetary Policy

This disagreement can occur because

■ the relationship between reserves and the money supply can change.

■ the relationship between the money supply and short-term interest rates can change.

■ velocity is not entirely stable.

■ it is difficult to determine which money supply measure is most appropriate to policy.

■ though today's monetary economists do not generally fall neatly into categories such as "Keynesian" and "monetarist," debates persist over the relative impact of monetary policy on prices and output. These relative impacts can change over time.

■ data are imperfect, and many data series are produced and transmitted with lags.

■ economic relationships are dynamic. Action the Fed takes today affects the economy well into the future.

1. What is monetary policy?

2. From 1998 to 2002, what was the dominant focus of monetary policy and why?

3. Explain why the money supply and short-term interest rates are inversely related.

4. What are some reasons for lags and imperfections in data used by central banks?

5. Why do many economists believe that central banks have more control over the price level than over real output?

6. What might cause velocity to change?

7. If velocity were extremely volatile, why would this complicate the job of making monetary policy?

8. What role does the money multiplier play in enabling the Fed to conduct monetary policy?

9. What is the fed funds rate?

10. What happens to the fed funds rate if the Fed follows a contractionary (tight money) policy?

11. What happens to the fed funds rate if the Fed follows an expansionary (easy money) policy?

12. Why do observers pay close attention to the federal funds rate?

Real Interest Rates and Nominal Interest Rates

If you bought a one-year bond for $1,000 and the bond paid an interest rate of 10 percent, at the end of the year would you be 10 percent wealthier? You will certainly have 10 percent more money than you did a year earlier, but can you buy 10 percent more? If the price level has risen, the answer is that you cannot buy 10 percent more: If the inflation rate were 8 percent, then you could buy only 2 percent more; if the inflation rate were 12 percent, you would be able to buy 2 percent less! The *nominal interest rate* is the rate the bank pays you on your savings or the rate that appears on your bond or car loan. The *actual real interest rate* represents the change in your purchasing power. The *expected real interest rate* represents the amount you need to receive in real terms to forgo consumption now for consumption in the future.

The relationship between the nominal interest rate, the real interest rate and the inflation rate can be written as

$$r = i - \pi$$

where r is the real interest rate, i is the nominal interest rate and π is the inflation rate. This relationship is called the *Fisher Equation*. In the example above with the 10 percent bond, if the inflation rate were 6 percent, then your real interest rate (the increase in your purchasing power) would be 4 percent.

Obviously banks and customers do not know what inflation is going to be, so the interest rates on loans, bonds, etc. are set based on expected inflation. The expected real interest rate is

$$r^e = i - \pi^e$$

where π^e is the expected inflation rate. The equation can be rewritten as

$$i = r^e + \pi^e$$

A bank sets the nominal interest rate equal to its expected real interest rate plus the expected inflation rate. However, the real interest rate it actually receives may be different if inflation is not equal to the bank's expected inflation rate.

The equation of exchange is MV = PQ. If we assume that velocity (V) is constant, then changes in the money supply (M) result in changes in the nominal output (PQ). The equation of exchange can be rewritten in terms of percentage change to be

percentage change in money supply + percentage change in velocity =
percentage change in price level + percentage change in real output

Activity written by Rae Jean B. Goodman, U.S. Naval Academy, Annapolis, Md.

The first term, *percentage change in the money supply,* is controlled by the monetary authority (Federal Reserve). Assuming that velocity is constant, the second term is zero. The third term is the inflation rate and the fourth term is the growth in real output. Output (Q) is determined by the factors of production, technology and the production function. Output can be taken as given. Therefore, the percentage change in the money supply results in an equal percentage change in the price level.

Increases in the money supply by the Federal Reserve will result in increases in the price level, or inflation. Using the Fisher Equation, the increase in inflation would result in an increase in the nominal interest rate or a decrease in the real interest rate or in some combination. This is known as the *Fisher Effect,* or *Fisher Hypothesis.* Evidence indicates that increases in the inflation rate result in increases in the nominal interest rate in the long run. Increases in the money supply are translated into increases in the price level and increases in the nominal interest rate *in the long run.*

We know that

■ in the short run, increases in the money supply decrease the nominal interest rate and real interest rate;

■ in the long run, increases in the money supply will result in an increase in the price level and the nominal interest rate.

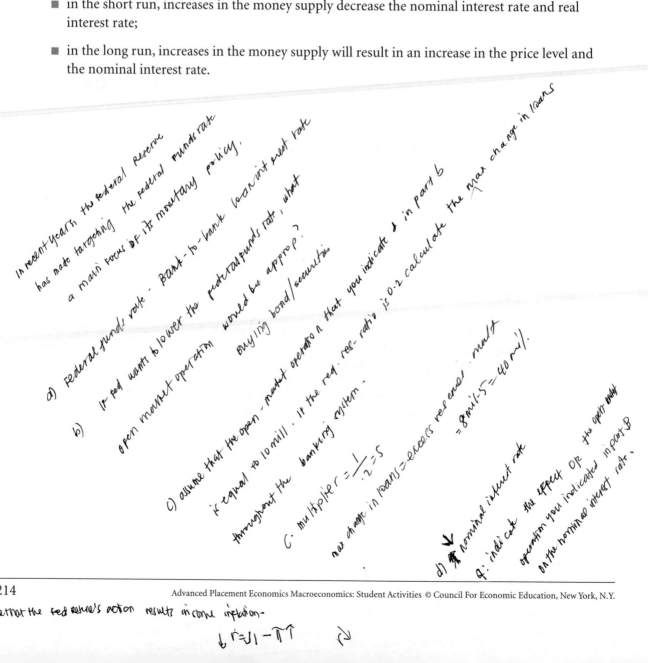

In recent years, the federal reserve has made targeting the federal funds rate a main focus of its monetary policy.

a) Federal funds rate - Bank-to-bank loan interest rate

b) If fed wants to lower the federal funds rate, what open market operation would be approp?
Buying bond/securities

c) assume that the open-market operation that you indicate d in part b is equal to 10 mill. If the req. res-ratio is 0.2 calculate the max change in loans throughout the banking system -

C- multiplier = $\frac{1}{.2}$ = 5

max change in loans = excess reserves · mult
= 8mil·5 = 40 mil.

d) nominal interest rate
d: indicate the effect OR the open market operation you indicated in part B on the nominal interest rate -

e) assume that the fed reserve's action results in some inflation -

$r = i - \pi$

Figure 41.1
Real and Nominal Interest Rates

Year	Nominal Interest Rate	Inflation Rate	Real Interest Rate
1991	5.41%	3.12%	
1992	3.46	2.30	
1993	3.02	2.42	
1994	4.27	2.05	
1995	5.51	2.12	
1996	5.02	1.87	
1997	5.07	1.85	
1998	4.78	1.14	
1999	4.64	1.56	
2000	5.82	2.29	
2001	3.39	1.96	

1. Figure 41.1 provides the nominal interest rates and inflation rates for the years 1991 through 2001.

   (A) Compute the actual real interest rates for 1991 through 2001.

   (B) Graph the nominal interest rates and the actual real interest rates on Figure 41.2.

 Figure 41.2
Real and Nominal Interest Rates

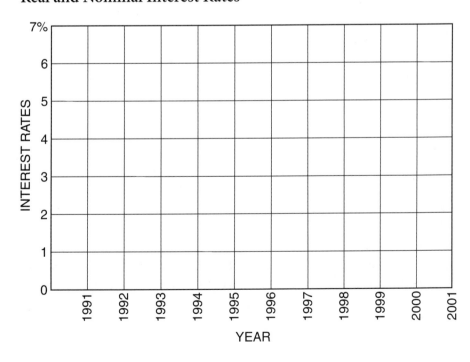

(C) Has the actual real interest rate stayed constant? _____

(D) If it has not, explain why you think the real rate has not been constant.

(E) For what years has the actual real interest rate remained nearly constant?

2. Frequently, economists argue that the monetary authorities should try to maintain a steady real interest rate. Explain why you think a steady real rate of interest is important to the economy.

 Figure 41.3
Expansionary Monetary Policy

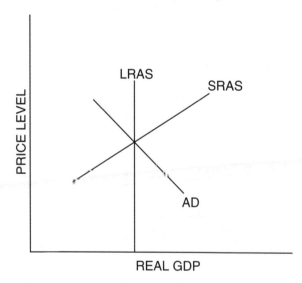

3. Suppose that initially the economy is at the intersection of AD and SRAS as shown in Figure 41.3. Now, the Fed decides to implement expansionary monetary policy to increase the level of employment.

(A) In the short run, what happens to real output? Explain why.

(B) In the short run, what happens to the price level? Explain why.

(C) In the short run, what happens to employment and nominal wages? Explain why.

(D) In the short run, what happens to nominal interest rates and real interest rates?

(E) In the long run, what happens to real output? Explain why.

(F) In the long run, what happens to the price level? Explain why.

(G) In the long run, what happens to employment and nominal wages? Explain why.

(H) In the long run, what happens to the nominal interest rate and the real interest rate?

Pusong
Lito

Monetary Policy

We now bring together all of the pieces of the process by which monetary policy is transmitted to the economy, and we examine both the short-run effects and the long-run effects of monetary policy.

✳ Figure 42.1
Effects of Monetary Policy

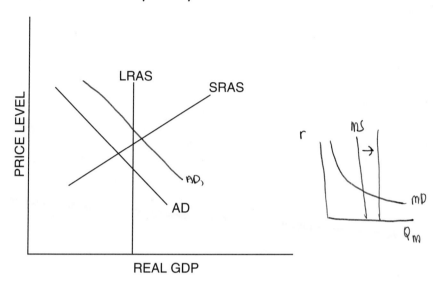

1. Suppose that initially the economy is at the intersection of AD and SRAS in Figure 42.1.

   (A) What monetary policy should the Fed implement to move the economy to full-employment output? _____Contractionary_____

   (B) If the Fed is going to use open market operations, it should *(buy / sell)* Treasury securities.

   (C) What is the effect on Treasury security (bond) prices?

   (D) In the short run, what is the effect on ~~nominal~~ *real* interest rates? Explain.

   The real interest rate would be decreased in the short run

   (E) In the short run, what happens to real output? Explain how the Fed's action results in a change in real output.

   The real output in the short run would be

   ↓r → ↑CM → ↑AD → ↑PL → ↑rGDP

Activity written by Rae Jean B. Goodman, U.S. Naval Academy, Annapolis, Md.
Activity written

wala ka man ngayon sa aking Piling.

(F) In the short run, what happens to the price level? Explain how the Fed's action results in a change to the price level.

Same as E.

 Figure 42.2
Moving to Full Employment

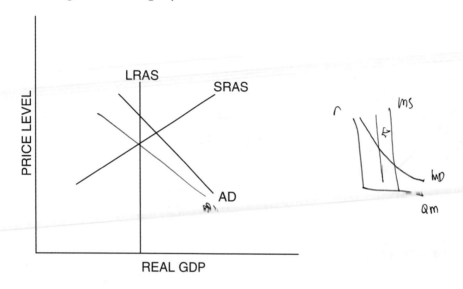

2. Suppose that initially the economy is at the intersection of AD and SRAS in Figure 42.2.

(A) What monetary policy should the Fed implement to move the economy to full-employment output? _____ Expansionary _____

(B) If the Fed is going to use open market operations, it should (buy / sell) Treasury securities.

(C) What is the effect on Treasury security (bond) prices?

(D) In the short run, what is the effect on ~~nominal~~ real interest rates? Explain.

The real interest rates in the short run would

Tr→↓CLI→↑AD
↑↓rGDP↑↓PL

(E) In the short run, what happens to real output? Explain how the Fed's action results in a change in real output.

The real output in the short run would

(F) In the short run, what happens to the price level? Explain how the Fed's action results in a change to the price level.

The price level in the short run

Figure 42.3
Expansionary Monetary Policy

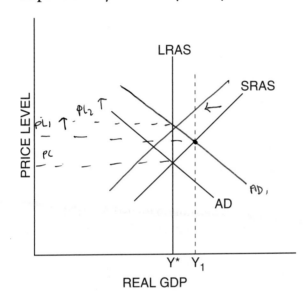

3. Suppose that in the situation shown in Figure 42.3, the aggregate supply and demand curves are represented by LRAS, SRAS and AD. The monetary authorities decide to maintain the level of employment represented by the output level Y_1 by using expansionary monetary policy.

(A) Explain the effect of the expansionary monetary policy on the price level and output in the short run.

↑ ms → ↓ r
↑ C ↑ I → ↑ AD
↑ PL ↑ rGDP

(B) Explain the effect on the price level and output in the long run.

↑ wages → ↓ SRAS
↑ PL → ↓ rGDP

Wala ka man ngayon sa aking piling.

nasasaktan man ang puso't damdamin, itkay mahal pa rin.

(C) Explain what you think will happen to the nominal rate of interest and the real rate of interest in the short run as the Fed continues to increase the money supply. Explain why.

PL will start to rise

(D) Explain what you think will happen to the nominal rate of interest and the real rate of interest in the long run. Explain why.

real r8 of intrst will stay low.

As PL ↑, nominal intrst r8s will start to rise.

4. Many economists think that moving from short-run equilibrium to long-run equilibrium may take several years. List three reasons why the economy might not immediately move to long-run equilibrium.

☐ takes wages a while to adjust

☐ prices take time to adjust

☐

5. In a short paragraph, summarize the long-run impact of an expansionary monetary policy on the economy.

↑ wages
↑ PL
— rGDP.

Advanced Placement Economics Macroeconomics: Student Activities © Council For Economic Education, New York, N.Y.

Sample Multiple-Choice Questions

Circle the letter of each correct answer.

1. The M1 definition of money includes which of the following?

    I.   Currency

    II. Deman~~d~~ ~~~~ ~~~~osits)

    ~~~~ deposits

[handwritten notes at left and center:]

1. D
2. B
3. D
4. E
5. D
6. B
7. C
8. B
9. D
10. D
11. A
12. C
13. E
14. A

15. D
16. D
17. A
18. D
19. B
20. E

the
~~~~er is
~~~~ =4

4. Whi~~ch~~ ~~~~ statements abou~~t~~ ~~~~ ~~feder~~al funds rate?

    I.   It is the same thing as the discount rate.

    II. It is the interest rate that banks charge each other for short-term loans.

    III. It is influenced by open market operations.

    (A) I only

    (B) II only

    (C) III only

    (D) I and II only

    (E) II and III only

5. Suppose the Federal Reserve buys $400,000 worth of securities from the securities dealers on the open market. If the reserve requirement is 20 percent and the banks hold no excess reserves, what will happen to the total money supply?

    (A) It will be unchanged.

    (B) It will contract by $2,000,000.

    (C) It will contract by $800,000.

    (D) It will expand by $2,000,000.

    (E) It will expand by $800,000.

6. The money market is definitely in equilibrium in which of the following cases?

    (A) When velocity is constant

    (B) When the quantity of money demanded equals the quantity of money supplied

    (C) When the present value is equal to the interest rate

    (D) When the present value is greater than the interest rate

    (E) When the interest rate is equal to the price of bonds

7. A commercial bank holds $500,000 in demand deposit liabilities and $120,000 in reserves. If the required reserve ratio is 20 percent, which of the following is the maximum amount by which this single commercial bank and the maximum amount by which the banking system can increase loans?

	Amount Created by Single Bank	Amount Created by Banking System
(A)	$5,000	$25,000
(B)	$20,000	$80,000
(C)	$20,000	$100,000
(D)	$30,000	$150,000
(E)	$120,000	$500,000

8. Which of the following does the Federal Reserve use most often to combat a recession?

    (A) Selling securities

    (B) Buying securities

    (C) Reducing the reserve requirement

    (D) Increasing the discount rate

    (E) Increasing the federal funds rate

9. To reduce inflation, the Federal Reserve could

    (A) expand the money supply in order to raise interest rates, which increases investment.

    (B) expand the money supply in order to lower interest rates, which increases investment.

    (C) contract the money supply in order to lower interest rates, which increases investment.

    (D) contract the money supply in order to raise interest rates, which decreases investment.

    (E) buy bonds and decrease the discount rate to encourage borrowing.

10. Reserves, the money supply and interest rates are most likely to change in which of the following ways when the Federal Reserve sells bonds?

	Reserves	Money Supply	Interest Rates
(A)	Increase	Increase	Increase
(B)	Increase	Increase	Decrease
(C)	Decrease	Increase	Decrease
(D)	Decrease	Decrease	Increase
(E)	Decrease	Decrease	Decrease

11. Which of the following actions by the Federal Reserve will result in an increase in banks' excess reserves?

    (A) Buying bonds on the open market

    (B) Selling bonds on the open market

    (C) Increasing the discount rate

    (D) Increasing the reserve requirement

    (E) Increasing the federal funds rate

12. Aggregate demand and aggregate supply analysis suggests that, in the short run, an expansionary monetary policy will result in

    (A) a shift in the aggregate demand curve to the left.

    (B) a shift in the aggregate supply curve to the left.

    (C) an increase in real GDP without much inflation when the economy is on the horizontal portion of the aggregate supply curve.

    (D) an increase in real GDP with high inflation when the economy is on the horizontal portion of the aggregate supply curve.

    (E) an increase in real GDP and no inflation when the economy is on the vertical portion of the aggregate supply curve.

13. Which of the following combinations of monetary policy actions would definitely cause a decrease in aggregate demand?

	Discount Rate	Open Market Operations	Reserve Requirement
(A)	Decrease	Buy bonds	Decrease
(B)	Decrease	Sell bonds	Decrease
(C)	Increase	Buy bonds	Increase
(D)	Increase	Sell bonds	Decrease
(E)	Increase	Sell bonds	Increase

14. Which of the following is most likely to increase the velocity of money?

    (A) Higher frequency of paychecks

    (B) Decrease in the price level

    (C) Decrease in interest rates

    (D) Decrease in personal income

    (E) Increase in the unemployment rate

look up: Expansionary & contractionary monetary policy.

15. Which of the following characteristics of money could be found in bars of gold?

(A) Portability, uniformity and stability in value

(B) Portability and acceptability

(C) Uniformity, acceptability and stability in value

(D) Uniformity and durability

(E) Portability and stability in value

16. The real interest rate is simply stated as the

(A) price of borrowed money in the future.

(B) inflation rate minus the CPI.

(C) nominal interest rate over time.

(D) nominal interest rate minus the expected inflation rate.

(E) nominal interest rate plus the expected inflation rate.

17. Vault cash and reserve accounts are similar in that each

(A) earns no interest.

(B) provides for the bank's use of large amounts of cash.

(C) is maintained by the bank at a fixed percentage set by the Federal Reserve.

(D) is kept on account at the Federal Reserve Bank.

(E) is part of the money supply.

18. The neutrality of money refers to the situation where

(A) money has not been the cause of war.

(B) increases in interest rates are matched by decreases in the price of bonds.

(C) increases in interest rates are matched by increases in the price of bonds.

(D) increases in the money supply eventually result in no change in real output.

(E) decreases in the money supply result in increases in the interest rate in the short run.

19. Expansionary monetary policy results in which of the following in the short run?
I. The money supply increases.
II. The nominal interest rate decreases.
III. The real interest rate decreases.
IV. Bond prices decrease.

(A) I and II only

(B) I, II and III only

(C) I, II and IV only

(D) III and IV only

(E) IV only

20. True statements about expansionary monetary policy in the long run include which of the following?
I. Price level increases to match the increase in the money supply.
II. The nominal interest rate equals the real interest rate plus the expected inflation rate.
III. The real output level has not permanently increased.

(A) I only

(B) II only

(C) III only

(D) I and II only

(E) I, II and III

↑taxes ↑govt spe.

Sample Short Free-Response Questions

*1. The reserve requirement for the banking system is 20 percent. Currently Third National Bank has no excess reserves. Then Behroz deposits $100 in her checking account at Third National.

(A) Explain, without using a mathematical formula, why Behroz's deposit can lead to an increase in the money supply that is greater than $100.

(B) Discuss two limitations of this process.

---

*Actual free-response question from a past AP test. Reprinted by permission of the College Entrance Examination Board, the copyright owner. For limited use by NCEE.

---

2. The Federal Reserve has three primary tools to expand or contract the money supply.

   (A) List the three tools.

   (B) Which tool does the Fed use most often?

   (C) Explain why the Federal Reserve uses the tool you indicated in Question 2(B).

3. Milton Friedman has said, "Inflation is primarily a monetary phenomenon."

   (A) Describe the conditions under which an increase in the money supply would be inflationary.

   (B) Use an aggregate supply and aggregate demand graph to show the conditions under which increases in the money supply are entirely inflationary.

4. Explain the statement that the Federal Reserve can "target" the size of the money supply or the interest rate, but not both.

5. Suppose the required reserve ratio is 0.20.

   (A) What would be the value of the deposit expansion multiplier? _____

   (B) Discuss why it is unlikely that a new deposit of $1,000 to a checking account would result in the money supply fully increasing as indicated by the deposit expansion multiplier.

6. Banks can borrow reserves at either the federal funds rate or at the discount rate.

   (A) Define the federal funds rate.

   (B) Define the discount rate.

   (C) Under what conditions would banks borrow at the discount rate?

Sample Long Free-Response Questions

1. Suppose the economy is experiencing rising unemployment, slowing increases in real GDP and modest inflation. The Federal Reserve decides to follow an expansionary policy.

   (A) Describe what this policy might include.

   (B) If the policy is effective, explain the short-run effect it would have on each of the following:
      (i) Interest rates
      (ii) Private investment
      (iii) GDP
      (iv) Employment

2. The Federal Reserve Board of Governors determines that it is currently appropriate to follow a contractionary policy.

(A) Use a correctly labeled aggregate demand and aggregate supply graph to illustrate the situation that would make this policy appropriate.

(B) Would the monetary policy be to increase or decrease the money supply? Explain.

(C) Describe the policy the Federal Reserve is likely to take, and explain how its action achieves the goal of following a contractionary policy. Explain how the policy would affect each of the following:

(i)   Interest rates
(ii) Investment
(iii) Output
(iv) Price level
(v)   Employment

3. Suppose the economy is at E in the graph below and the Federal Reserve decides to implement expansionary monetary policy to reduce the unemployment rate.

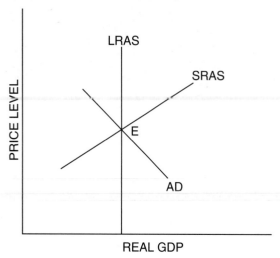

(A) Explain the short-run effect of the expansionary policy on each of the following:
   (i)   Nominal interest rates
   (ii) Real interest rates
   (iii) Output
   (iv) Price level
   (v)   Employment

(B) Explain the long-run effect of the expansionary policy on each of the following:
   (i)   Output
   (ii) Price
   (iii) Employment
   (iv) Nominal interest rates
   (v)   Real interest rates

Macroeconomics | Unit 5

Monetary and Fiscal Policy Combinations: Stabilization Policy in the Real World

■ Macroeconomic policy involves combinations of fiscal and monetary policies.

■ The inside lag is the amount of time it takes policy makers to recognize the economic situation and take action. The outside or impact lag is the amount of time it takes the economy to respond to the policy changes. The inside lag is long for fiscal policy and short for monetary policy. The outside lag is very short for fiscal policy and variable for monetary policy.

■ Crowding-out is the effect on investment and consumption spending of an increase in interest rates caused by increased borrowing by the federal government. The higher interest rates crowd out business and consumer borrowing.

■ A Phillips curve illustrates the trade-off between inflation and unemployment. The trade-off differs in the short and long run, varies at different times and is often different for increases and decreases in output.

■ The short-run Phillips curve shows a trade-off between the inflation rate and the unemployment rate.

■ The long-run Phillips curve is vertical.

■ Both monetary and fiscal policies are primarily aggregate demand policies, but not all of the macroeconomic problems in the economy are aggregate demand problems.

■ If factors other than excess aggregate demand are contributing to inflation, it is difficult for monetary policy to control inflation.

■ The Barro-Ricardo effect is the possibility that government deficits will lead to an increase in private savings and a decrease in consumption, thus offsetting the effects of expansionary fiscal policy.

■ Economic growth is concerned with increasing an economy's total productive capacity at full employment or its natural rate of output. This output is represented by a vertical long-run aggregate supply curve.

■ Economic growth can be shown graphically as a rightward shift of a nation's long-run aggregate supply curve or a rightward shift of its production possibilities curve.

■ Short-run economic growth is usually measured by changes in real gross domestic product or by changes in real GDP per capita.

■ The rate of economic growth is affected by a variety of aggregate supply and aggregate demand factors.

■ Different economic theories are only one reason why economists disagree. Other reasons are different assumptions, different values, different interpretations about economic history and different ideas about policy lags.

Monetary and Fiscal Policy

Part A
Tools of Monetary and Fiscal Policy

Both monetary and fiscal policy can be used to influence the inflation rate and real output. Indicate what effect each specific policy has on inflation and real output in the short run (nine to 18 months).

Figure 43.1

Monetary Policy	Inflation	Real Output
1. (A) Buy government securities		
(B) Sell government securities		
2. (A) Decrease the discount rate		
(B) Increase the discount rate		
3. (A) Decrease reserve requirement		
(B) Increase reserve requirement		

Fiscal Policy	Inflation	Real Output
4. (A) Increase government spending		
(B) Decrease government spending		
5. (A) Increase taxes		
(B) Decrease taxes		

Part B
Lags in Policy Making

As the economic situation changes, policy makers must decide when to take action and which policy action to take. Then they must implement the policy. The economy then responds to the policy. The amount of time it takes policy makers to recognize and take action is called the *inside lag*. The amount of time it takes the economy to respond to the policy changes is called the *outside* or *impact lag*. The inside lag is estimated to be short for monetary policy but long for fiscal policy. The inside lag is long for fiscal policy because the legislative branch must come to agreement about the appropriate action. The outside lag, however, is long and variable for monetary policy but very short for fiscal policy.

6. Explain why the inside lag can be short for monetary policy but the outside lag is long and variable.

Activity written by Rae Jean B. Goodman, U.S. Naval Academy, Annapolis, Md.

---

7. Explain why the outside lag is short for fiscal policy.

8. Explain why lags are important to the discussion of stabilization policy.

Crowding-Out: A Graphical Representation

Monetary policy and fiscal policy do not exist in separate airtight compartments. Monetary policy and fiscal policy can reinforce or accommodate each other, or they can work at cross-purposes. This activity assumes no changes in the foreign exchange rate, imports or exports.

For example, an expansionary fiscal policy will increase aggregate demand. The expansionary fiscal policy should also increase the demand for money. If the Fed does not increase the money supply, interest rates will rise. Because the government is borrowing money to finance its expansionary fiscal policy, consumers and businesses will be crowded-out of the financial markets. This could lower consumer and investment spending and slow down the economic expansion. On the other hand, if the Fed increases the money supply, interest rates should not rise as much. Of course, increasing the money supply will increase the price level further.

Part A
Using Aggregate Demand and Aggregate Supply Analysis

 Figure 44.1
Crowding-Out Using Aggregate Demand and Aggregate Supply Analysis

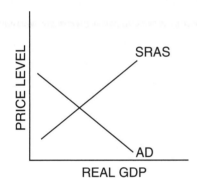 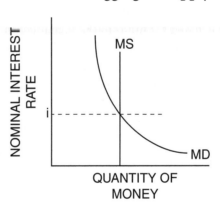

1. Assume fiscal policy is expansionary and monetary policy keeps the stock of money constant at MS. Shift one curve in each graph to illustrate the effect of the fiscal policy.

    (A) Which curve did you shift in the short-run aggregate demand and aggregate supply graph? What happens as a result of this new curve?

    (B) In the money market graph, which curve did you shift to demonstrate the effect of the fiscal policy? What happens as a result of this shift?

Adapted from Phillip Saunders, *Introduction to Macroeconomics: Student Workbook,* 18th ed. (Bloomington, Ind., 1998). Copyright 1998 Phillip Saunders. All rights reserved. Activity revised by Rae Jean B. Goodman, U.S. Naval Academy, Annapolis, Md.

(C) Given the change in interest rates, what happens in the short-run aggregate supply and aggregate demand graph?

(D) How could a monetary policy action prevent the changes in interest rates and output you identified in (B) and (C)? Shift a curve in the money market graph, and explain how this shift would reduce crowding-out.

Part B
Using the Loanable Funds Market

The loanable funds market provides another approach to looking at the effects of increases in the budget deficit. The *demand* for funds in the loanable funds market comes from the private sector (business investment and consumer borrowing), the government sector (budget deficits) and the foreign sector. The *supply* of funds in the loanable funds market comes from private savings (businesses and households), the government sector (budget surpluses), the Federal Reserve (money supply) and the foreign sector.

 Figure 44.2
Loanable Funds Market

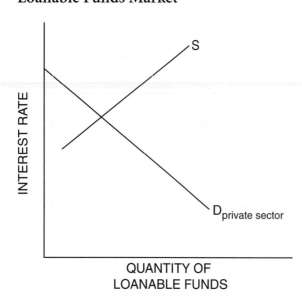

2. Shift one of the curves on Figure 44.2 to indicate what occurs in the loanable funds market if government spending increases without any increases in tax revenue or the money supply.

(A) What happens to the interest rate as a result of this expansionary fiscal policy? Explain.

(B) Indicate on the graph the new quantity of private demand for loanable funds.

(C) An accommodating monetary policy could prevent the effects you described in (A) and (B). Shift a curve in the diagram to show how the accommodating monetary policy would counteract the effects of crowding-out. Explain what would happen to interest rates and the level of private demand for loanable funds as a result of this new curve.

Part C
Applications

3. Indicate whether you agree (A), disagree (D) or are uncertain (U) about the truth of the following statement and explain your reasoning. "Exhaustion of excess bank reserves inevitably puts a ceiling on every business boom because without money the boom cannot continue."

Answer the questions that follow each of the scenarios below.

4. The Federal Reserve Open Market Committee wishes to accommodate or reinforce a contractionary fiscal policy.

   (A) Would the Fed buy bonds, sell bonds or neither?

   (B) What effect would this policy have on bond prices and interest rates?

   (C) What effect would this policy have on bank reserves and the money supply?

   (D) What effect would this policy have on the quantity of loanable funds demanded by the private sector?

   (E) What effect would the change in interest rates you identified in (B) have on aggregate demand?

5. The Federal Reserve Open Market Committee wishes to accommodate or reinforce an expansionary fiscal policy.

   (A) Would the Fed buy bonds, sell bonds or neither?

   (B) What effect would this policy have on bond prices and interest rates?

   (C) What effect would this policy have on bank reserves and the money supply?

   (D) What effect would this policy have on the quantity of loanable funds demanded by the private sector?

   (E) What effect would the change in interest rates you identified in (B) have on aggregate demand?

Graphing Monetary and Fiscal Policy Interactions

Illustrate the short-run effects for each monetary and fiscal policy combination using aggregate demand and supply curves, the money market and the loanable funds market. Once again, assume that there are no changes in the foreign sector. Circle the appropriate symbols (↑ for increase, ↓ for decrease, and ? for uncertain), and explain the effect of the policies on real GDP, the price level, unemployment, interest rates and investment.

1. The unemployment rate is 10 percent, and the CPI is increasing at a 2 percent rate. The federal government cuts personal income taxes and increases its spending. The Fed buys bonds on the open market.

✳ Figure 45.1
Expansionary Monetary and Fiscal Policy

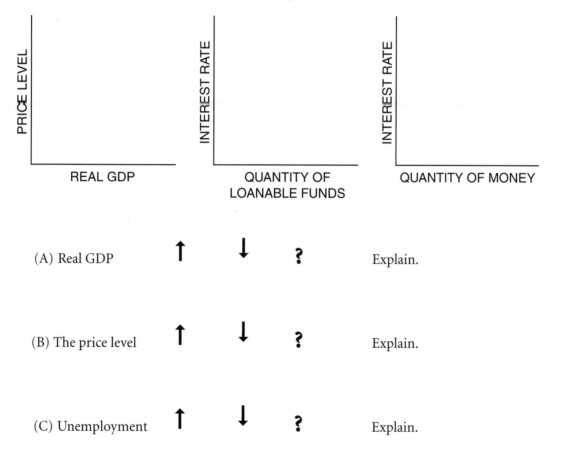

(A) Real GDP	↑	↓	?	Explain.
(B) The price level	↑	↓	?	Explain.
(C) Unemployment	↑	↓	?	Explain.

Activity written by John Morton, National Council on Economic Education, New York, N.Y., with modifications by Rae Jean B. Goodman, U.S. Naval Academy, Annapolis, Md.

(D) Interest rates   ↑   ↓   **?**   Explain.

(E) Investment   ↑   ↓   **?**   Explain.

2. The unemployment rate is 6 percent, and the CPI is increasing at a 9 percent rate. The federal government raises personal income taxes and cuts spending. The Federal Reserve sells bonds on the open market.

✳ Figure 45.2

Contractionary Monetary and Fiscal Policy

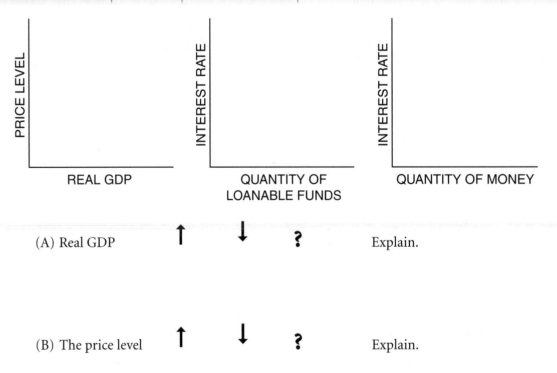

(A) Real GDP   ↑   ↓   **?**   Explain.

(B) The price level   ↑   ↓   **?**   Explain.

Advanced Placement Economics Macroeconomics: Student Activities © Council For Economic Education, New York, N.Y.

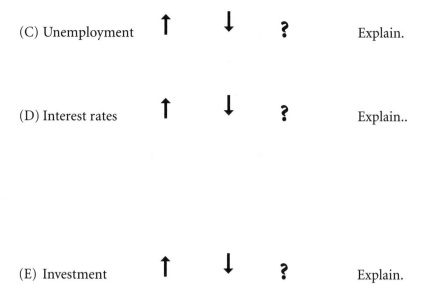

(C) Unemployment ↑ ↓ ? Explain.

(D) Interest rates ↑ ↓ ? Explain..

(E) Investment ↑ ↓ ? Explain.

3. The unemployment rate is 6 percent, and the CPI is increasing at a 5 percent rate. The federal government cuts personal-income taxes and maintains current spending. The Fed sells bonds on the open market.

Figure 45.3
Contractionary Monetary Policy and Expansionary Fiscal Policy

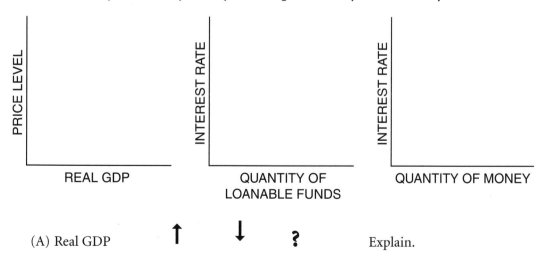

(A) Real GDP ↑ ↓ ? Explain.

(B) The price level   ↑   ↓   ?   Explain.

(C) Unemployment   ↑   ↓   ?   Explain.

(D) Interest rates   ↑   ↓   ?   Explain.

(E) Investment   ↑   ↓   ?   Explain.

Short-Run Phillips Curve

A.W. Phillips studied the historical relationship between the rate of change in wages and the unemployment rate in the United Kingdom. In 1958 he published his findings, showing an inverse relationship between these variables. In following studies, other economists found that the inverse relationship held when a change in the level of prices (inflation) was used in place of the rate of change in wages. In other words, when inflation increased, the unemployment rate decreased; and when inflation decreased, the unemployment rate increased. A graphic representation of this trade-off became known as the *Phillips curve*.

In Figure 46.1, an example of the Phillips curve illustrates the trade-off between inflation and unemployment, or all of the different possible combinations of inflation and unemployment that exist along the curve.

✳ Figure 46.1
Phillips Curve

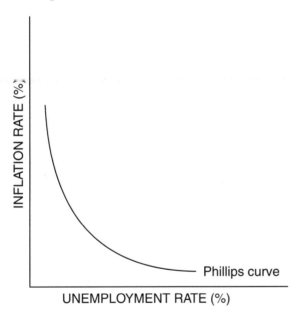

The economy of the 1960s appeared to support Phillips' hypothesis. The economy was sluggish, inflation was low and the unemployment rate was high. Since the unemployment rate was higher than the natural rate of unemployment, the economy was not operating at its potential GDP. The Phillips curve suggested to some economists that if policy makers wished to lower unemployment, the trade-off would be higher inflation.

Activity written by Joanne Benjamin, Los Gatos High School, Los Gatos, Calif.

---

1. Suppose government policy makers want to increase GDP because the economy is not operating at its potential. They can increase aggregate demand by increasing government spending, lowering taxes or a combination of both. Using an AD and SRAS model, draw a new AD curve that will represent the change caused by government policy designed to increase real GDP.

 Figure 46.2
Expansionary Fiscal Policy

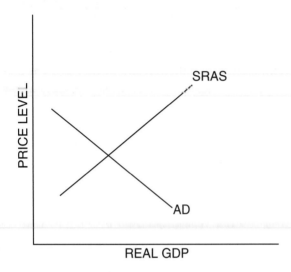

(A) What happens to the price level in the short run? _____

(B) What happens to real GDP in the short run? _____

(C) What happens to the rate of unemployment in the short run? _____

(D) The Federal Reserve can use monetary policy to try to stimulate the economy. It can encourage bank lending by _____ bonds on the open market, _____ the discount rate and/or _____ the reserve requirements.

A Phillips curve would tell the same story. Inflation is low at high levels of unemployment, but inflation begins to increase as the unemployment rate decreases. The Phillips curve is useful for analyzing short-run movements of unemployment and inflation. See Figure 46.3.

Figure 46.3
Short-Run Phillips Curve

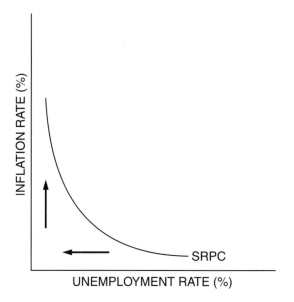

In the late 1960s, some economists such as Milton Friedman and Edmund Phelps published papers that concluded there were two Phillips curves: one for the short run and one for the long run. The controversy continued as the economy of the 1970s experienced high inflation and high unemployment at the same time. The relationship appeared to be less stable than previously thought; the short-run Phillips curve had shifted to the right.

 Figure 46.4
**Short-Run Phillips Curve
During the 1960s and 1970s**

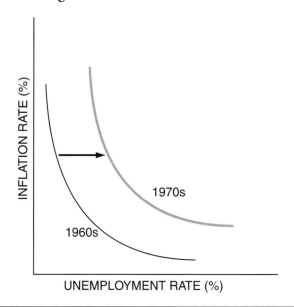

2. Aggregate supply shocks resulting from the oil embargo imposed by Middle Eastern countries (OPEC) and worldwide crop failures helped to bring about higher inflation and higher unemployment rates. The economy, with rising prices and decreased output, was in a state of *stagflation*. Using an AD and SRAS model, draw a new SRAS curve that will represent the change caused by the OPEC oil embargo.

 Figure 46.5
Effects of Oil Embargo

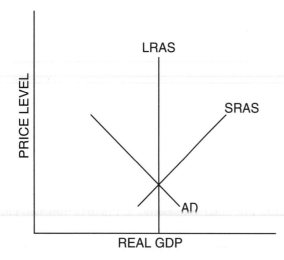

(A) In the short run, based on the new SRAS,

   (i)   what happens to the price level? _____

   (ii) what happens to real GDP? _____

   (iii) what happens to the rate of unemployment? _____

(B) As the economy moves to the long run,

   (i)   what happens to the wage rate?

   (ii) what happens to the price level?

   (iii) what happens to real GDP?

   (iv) what happens to the rate of unemployment?

Advanced Placement Economics Macroeconomics: Student Activities © Council For Economic Education, New York, N.Y.

3. Use the AD and SRAS model in Figure 46.6 to show the appropriate policy response to the oil-price increases in the following instances. Be sure to show on the graph the effects of the oil-price increase.

(A) If unemployment were the main concern of policy makers

(B) If inflation were the main concern of policy makers

(C) If inflation and unemployment were of equal concern

 Figure 46.6
Policy Response to Oil Embargo

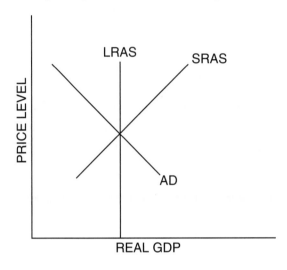

4. As inflation in the 1970s continued to increase, economists argued that, for a reduction in money growth to be fully effective in lowering inflation, the Federal Reserve would need to convince people it was serious about reducing money growth — in other words, the Fed would stick with a lower money growth policy until inflation decreased. Why would it be important for the Fed to establish this credibility?

5. In 1980, the unemployment rate was no lower than it had been in 1960, but inflation was much higher. Between 1980 and 1982, the economy experienced a recession and unemployment rose. Explain the general effect of a recession on unemployment and inflation. Then explain why the recession of 1980-82 was accompanied by high inflation.

6. Eventually the OPEC cartel was weakened, and energy prices decreased. Several U.S. industries, including communications and transportation, were deregulated. This caused greater competition. Explain and illustrate the effects of a weakened oil cartel and deregulation using both the aggregate demand and aggregate supply model and the Phillips curve.

Economic Growth and the Determinants of Productive Capacity

The limit of an economy's ability to produce real goods and services is set by the quantity and quality of its basic productive resources and technology. At any given moment, an economy's total productive capacity may be fixed, but over time an economy can increase (or decrease) its capacity to produce real goods and services by increasing (or decreasing) the quantity and/or the quality of its productive resources.

An economy's productive resources can be classified in several different ways. Some of our resources are physical or tangible: things that we can see, count, weigh or measure. Other resources that are useful in the production process are intangible. Intangible resources are more difficult to identify and measure, but no less important than tangible resources.

At any given time, an economy's productive capacity is determined by the quantity and quality of its

- **Human Resources:** labor resources, but not all labor is equal. Different people have different skills, based on their investment in *human capital*. Human capital (education and skill level) and entrepreneurship are difficult to measure.

- **Natural Resources:** the gifts of nature that are useful in producing goods and services. There are fixed, exhaustible and renewable natural resources.

- **Capital Goods:** the plant, equipment and machinery needed to make other goods and services

- **Technological Progress:** when production becomes more efficient, producing more output without using any more inputs: additional capital or labor

- **Public Policy:** the basic social, economic, legal and political values and institutions supported by a society that either aid or hinder efficient markets and the production of goods and services

In practice, economic growth is usually measured by changes in real GDP or, better still, changes in real GDP per capita: gross domestic product per person adjusted for changes in prices. The rate of economic growth is the average annual percentage change in real GDP per capita. Economists use real GDP per capita to measure living standards across time and between countries.

To summarize, economic growth occurs because an economy experiences technical progress, increased investments in physical capital and increased investments in human capital. In the most fundamental sense, economic growth is concerned with increasing an economy's total productive capacity at full employment.

Adapted from Phillip Saunders, *Introduction to Macroeconomics: Student Workbook,* 18th ed. (Bloomington, Ind., 1998). Copyright 1998 Phillip Saunders. All rights reserved. Activity revised by Elaine McBeth, College of William and Mary, Williamsburg, Va.

Part A
Measuring Economic Growth in Hamilton County and Jefferson County

 Figure 47.1

Year	Hamilton Real GDP	Hamilton Population	Jefferson Real GDP	Jefferson Population
1	$2.1 billion	70,000	$500,000	15
2	2.5 billion	80,000	525,000	16
3	2.8 billion	90,000	600,000	17
4	2.7 billion	86,000	650,000	18

1. Using Figure 47.1 as a reference, fill out the tables in Figures 47.2, 47.3 and 47.4.

 Figure 47.2

Time period	Hamilton % Change in Real GDP	Jefferson % Change in Real GDP
From Year 1 to Year 2		
From Year 2 to Year 3		
From Year 3 to Year 4		

 Figure 47.3

Year	Hamilton Per Capita Real GDP	Jefferson Per Capita Real GDP
1		
2		
3		
4		

* Figure 47.4

Time period	Hamilton % Change in Per Capita Real GDP	Jefferson % Change in Per Capita Real GDP
From Year 1 to Year 2		
From Year 2 to Year 3		
From Year 3 to Year 4		

2. When did Hamilton County experience the largest growth in real GDP? _____

    In per capita real GDP? _____

    Are these growth rates different? Explain.

3. When did Jefferson County experience the largest growth in real GDP? _____

    In per capita real GDP? _____

    Are these growth rates different? Explain.

4. The residents of Hamilton County believe they live in a wealthier community than small rural Jefferson County. Based on these numbers, do they? Explain.

Part B
Analyzing the Reasons for Economic Growth

Economic growth can be illustrated by a rightward shift of the long-run aggregate supply curve or a shift outward of the production possibilities curve of consumption goods vs. capital goods.

5. Draw a graph that includes AD, SRAS and LRAS and then draw a graph of a PPC.

 Figure 47.5
Relationship Between LRAS and PPC:
Increased Investment in Education

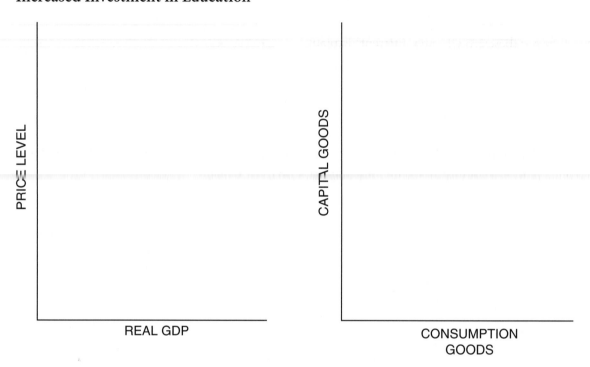

(A) On each graph you drew, show the effect of an increased investment in education that makes the work force more productive. Explain your reasoning.

(B) Of the five factors that affect economic growth, which factor is increased by this investment in education?

6. Explain how fewer government regulations will affect economic growth. Cite an example to support your explanation. Show the effect of fewer government regulations on the graphs in Figure 47.6.

 Figure 47.6
Relationship Between LRAS and PPC:
Fewer Government Regulations

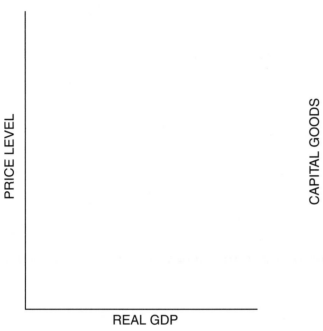
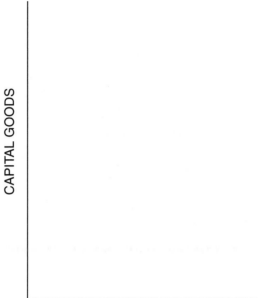

7. Briefly explain how the following policies will affect economic growth and why.

   (A) Higher taxes on businesses

(B) Improvements in technology

(C) Less savings by people who want to enjoy the good life

(D) Higher productivity of labor because of improved management styles

(E) Lower interest rates

Why Economists Disagree

Part A
Understanding the Reasons Why Economists Disagree

It is not unusual to find "experts" disagreeing with each other. Experts disagree about all sorts of matters: nuclear power, environmental protection and who will win the Super Bowl. Why do experts disagree? How can the average person make sense out of the differing viewpoints and recommendations? Here are several important factors that often lead economists to different conclusions.

■ Different Time Periods

One economist might state that the current policy of the government will lead to inflation. Another might disagree. Both could be right if they are talking about the effects of the policy on inflation at different times — for example, six months from now compared with two years from now.

■ Different Assumptions

Because an economy is a complex system, it is often hard to predict the effects of a particular policy or event. Therefore, to be able to make predictions, economists usually must make certain assumptions. But economists often differ in their assumptions. For example, one economist might assume that the federal budget deficit will become larger next year. Another might not. These different assumptions could be the result of their assumptions about economic growth, tax revenue and government spending.

■ Different Economic Theories

Economists agree on many matters such as, "If the price of beef goes up and nothing else changes, people will buy less beef." This is a prediction with which nearly all economists would agree because it rests on the generally accepted law of demand. However, economists have yet to settle a number of important questions, especially those concerning macroeconomics. Macroeconomics deals with the behavior of the economy as a whole or large subdivisions of it, and how to influence this behavior. Economists have several different theories or explanations about what influences macroeconomic behavior. Until these theories are reconciled or until one of them is widely agreed on as best, economists will disagree on macroeconomic questions because the economists are using different theories. The same applies to certain microeconomic questions.

■ Different Values

Economics is concerned with explaining what is happening in the economy. It is also concerned with predictions. The economist should be able to say to the president or to Congress, "If you follow Policy One, then X, Y and Z will happen. If you follow Policy Two, then Q, R and S will happen. Pick the policy that gives the results you like better." In practice, such statements by economists often contain more than just analysis and a prediction about results. Their statements often recommend policies they like because the results agree with their own values — in other words, the results they prefer. For

From *Master Curriculum Guide in Economics: Teaching Strategies for High School Economics Courses* (New York: National Council on Economic Education, 1985), p. 158. Modified by John Morton, National Council on Economic Education, New York, N.Y.

example, some economists will recommend Policy One because X, Y and Z will happen and they favor achieving X, Y and Z. Other economists will recommend Policy Two because they favor achieving results Q, R and S. Such disagreements are basically about which outcomes the economists prefer. The economic policies they recommend are determined by their preferred outcomes.

Part B
Listening in on a Discussion of Economists

Four distinguished professors of economics are discussing current economic policy at a luncheon press conference attended by leading reporters of business news. Let's listen in.

Professor T.X. Cut: Let's separate issues. On the fiscal policy side, this administration's budget proposal is not extravagant or inflationary. The tax cuts are partly balanced by spending cuts. With so many people still unemployed and many factories still closed, a policy of this kind cannot rekindle inflation. The tax cuts will stimulate consumer spending, work effort and business investment in an economy just emerging from a recession. We must let people keep the fruits of their labor and sustain savings as incentives to produce and invest more. The spending cuts will prevent government from continuing to receive an ever-increasing piece of the nation's economic pie.

Professor U.R. Nutts: Excuse me, Dr. Cut. But that position makes little sense. First of all, let me say that this administration's tax cuts and spending cuts have been and are grossly unfair. The tax cuts have favored the rich, and the spending cuts have reduced programs that help maintain economic security for Americans with low incomes. The present deficit — and the deficits projected for the future — are so large that they threaten our recovery from the recession. Here's why: All deficits must be paid for by government borrowing, and because the government is borrowing so much money, there is less available for consumers and businesses. With government borrowing now threatening to increase, interest rates will rise and this will reduce spending for houses and cars and, in fact, spending on anything bought with a loan, as well as business investment that must be financed by borrowing. In other words, some important private borrowing will be crowded-out. Sometime next year, the recovery will therefore weaken, and we'll move back into recession. Taxes should be raised, especially on the wealthy, and at least some government programs that help low-income people should be restored to the original funding levels.

Professor E.Z. Money: Let me just comment, U.R., on your point about federal spending and borrowing crowding-out private consumer spending and business investment. This is where monetary policy comes in. The Federal Reserve must continue to allow relatively free expansion of money and credit. If the Fed makes more money available, there will be less pressure for interest rates to rise. We'll be able to sustain the recovery in housing, autos and other sectors. And businesses will be able to get loans for investments at affordable interest rates. Continuing our economic growth by sustaining this recovery is the most important task we have before us. Increasing taxes now would only reduce total spending and thus threaten the recovery.

Professor Fred Critic: Excuse me, Dr. Money. You forget that the expansion of the money supply we're currently witnessing is part of a long history of bungling by the monetary policy makers. Our most recent recession was brought on by the Fed's jamming on the monetary brakes by an abrupt reduction in the increase of the money supply in order to bring inflation under control. They overdid it, as they always do, and produced a recession. Now, they're overdoing it in the other direction: stepping on the monetary accelerator and increasing the money supply too rapidly. This will stimulate the economy all right, but in a year or two these actions will rekindle inflation. The Fed then will again jam on the monetary brakes and produce yet another recession. Everyone knows this. Interest rates right now are higher than they should be because everyone expects more inflation later. Only moderate growth in the money supply can bring interest rates down in the long run. The only way to get back on a long-term, stable economic growth path is to reduce money growth to a steady, predictable, noninflationary level.

Ladies and gentlemen, that's all the time we have. Let's give our distinguished panel a round of applause.

Part C
Analyzing Disagreements Among Economists

Economists disagree for the following reasons:

- Because they evaluate the impact of policy over different lengths of time.

- Because they make different assumptions.

- Because they have different theories about how the economy works.

- Because they have different values and ideas about which economic goals are most important.

Now analyze each professor's comments in Part B, using the format on the next two pages.

Professor T.X. Cut

Major point:

Time period:

Assumptions:

Theoretical support:

Values:

Professor U.R. Nutts

Major point:

Time period:

Assumptions:

Theoretical support:

Values:

Advanced Placement Economics Macroeconomics: Student Activities © Council For Economic Education, New York, N.Y.

Professor E.Z. Money

Major point:

Time period:

Assumptions:

Theoretical support:

Values:

Professor Fred Critic

Major point:

Time period:

Assumptions:

Theoretical support:

Values:

Sample Multiple-Choice Questions

Circle the letter of each correct answer.

1. Which of the following monetary and fiscal policy combinations would definitely cause a decrease in aggregate demand in the short run?

	Discount Rate	Government Spending	Open Market Operations
(A)	Decrease	Decrease	Buy bonds
(B)	Decrease	Increase	Buy bonds
(C)	Decrease	Increase	Sell bonds
(D)	Increase	Decrease	Sell bonds
(E)	Increase	Decrease	Buy bonds

2. Which of the following monetary and fiscal policy combinations would definitely cause an increase in aggregate demand?

	Reserve Requirements	Taxes	Government Spending
(A)	Decrease	Decrease	Decrease
(B)	Decrease	Decrease	Increase
(C)	Increase	Decrease	Increase
(D)	Increase	Increase	Decrease
(E)	Increase	Decrease	Decrease

3. Assume that the economy has a low unemployment rate and a high rate of inflation. Which of the following sets of monetary and fiscal policies would be consistent and designed to reduce the rate of inflation?

	Discount Rate	Government Spending	Open Market Operations
(A)	Increase	Increase	Buy bonds
(B)	Increase	Increase	Sell bonds
(C)	Increase	Decrease	Sell bonds
(D)	Increase	Decrease	Buy bonds
(E)	Decrease	Decrease	Buy bonds

4. To counter the crowding-out effect on interest rates caused by the government's deficit spending, the Federal Reserve can
   (A) cut tax rates.
   (B) increase tax rates.
   (C) increase the discount rate.
   (D) increase the reserve requirement.
   (E) buy bonds through open market operations.

5. Which of the following would best portray long-run economic growth?
   (A) A leftward shift of the aggregate demand curve
   (B) A rightward shift of the aggregate demand curve
   (C) A leftward shift of the production possibilities curve
   (D) A leftward shift of the long-run aggregate supply curve
   (E) A rightward shift of the long-run aggregate supply curve

6. An increase in which of the following would be most likely to increase long-run economic growth?
   (A) Taxes
   (B) Interest rates
   (C) Consumer spending
   (D) Productivity
   (E) Value of domestic currency

7. An expansionary fiscal policy will result in an increase in the interest rate unless which of the following occurs?

(A) Taxes are cut instead of government expenditures being increased.

(B) The money supply is increased.

(C) Wage and price controls are imposed.

(D) The exchange rate is fixed.

(E) The Federal Reserve sells government bonds.

8. An expansionary monetary policy may promote long-run growth if it leads to

(A) an increase in consumption.

(B) an increase in investment.

(C) an increase in government spending.

(D) a constant level of government spending.

(E) a decrease in net exports.

9. If the government increases spending without a tax increase and simultaneously no monetary-policy changes are made, which of the following would most likely occur?

(A) Income would not rise at all because no new money is available for increased consumer spending.

(B) The rise in income may be greater than the multiplier would predict because the higher interest rates will stimulate investment spending.

(C) The rise in income may be smaller than the multiplier would predict because the higher interest rates will crowd-out private investment spending.

(D) Income will go up by exactly the amount of the new government spending since this acts as a direct injection to the income stream.

(E) Income will not go up unless taxes are cut as well.

10. If Congress and the Federal Reserve both wished to encourage growth of productive capacity in an economy already close to full employment, it would be most appropriate to

(A) increase interest rates by buying bonds on the open market.

(B) use a tight money policy to decrease government spending.

(C) reduce taxes on consumption, increase income taxes and increase government transfer payments.

(D) reduce interest rates by engaging in open-market operations and raise taxes on personal income.

(E) increase capital gains taxes and decrease the money supply.

11. "Sales of durable goods last month were surprisingly high. Recent price increases have pushed the CPI to more than a 7 percent increase for the past year. On average, the producer price index has gained 1 percent each month during the last year. Wage rates have increased throughout the economy, but productivity gains are minimal. The unemployment rate, however, is steady at 6 percent." Which of the following changes in the tax rate, government spending and the federal funds rate are most appropriate given the state of the economy?

	Tax Rate	Government Spending	Federal Funds Rate
(A)	Increase	Increase	Increase
(B)	Increase	Decrease	Increase
(C)	Increase	Decrease	Decrease
(D)	Decrease	Increase	Decrease
(E)	Decrease	Decrease	Decrease

12. When the unemployment rate is 10 percent and the CPI is rising at 2 percent, the federal government cuts taxes and increases government spending. If the Federal Reserve buys bonds on the open market, interest rates, investment, real gross domestic product (GDP) and the price level are most likely to change in which of the following ways?

	Interest Rates	Invest-ment	Real GDP	Price Level
(A)	Decrease	Decrease	Increase	Increase
(B)	Decrease	Increase	Increase	Increase
(C)	Increase	Decrease	Decrease	Decrease
(D)	Increase	Decrease	Increase	Increase
(E)	Increase	Increase	Increase	Increase

13. When the unemployment rate is 4.5 percent and the CPI is rising at a 12 percent rate, the federal government raises taxes and cuts government spending. If the Federal Reserve sells bonds on the open market, interest rates, investment, real gross domestic product (GDP) and the price level are most likely to change in which of the following ways?

	Interest Rates	Invest-ment	Real GDP	Price Level
(A)	Decrease	Decrease	Increase	Increase
(B)	Increase	Decrease	Increase	Increase
(C)	Increase	Decrease	Decrease	Decrease
(D)	Decrease	Increase	Increase	Increase
(E)	Decrease	Decrease	Increase	Increase

14. The statement that "the cost of reducing the rate of inflation is that people must lose their jobs" indicates that the speaker believes in a relationship that is usually depicted by which of the following?

(A) The short-run Phillips curve

(B) The liquidity trap

(C) The production function

(D) The quantity theory of money

(E) The spending multiplier

15. In the short run, combining an expansionary fiscal policy with a tight money policy is most likely to cause

(A) real GDP to increase.

(B) real GDP to decrease.

(C) interest rates to fall.

(D) interest rates to rise.

(E) the federal budget deficit to decrease.

Use the following graph to answer questions 16 and 17.

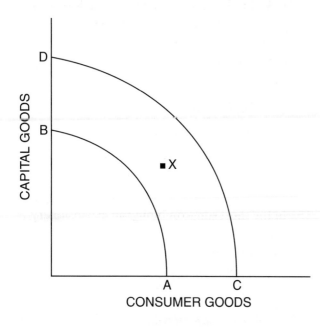

16. If the production possibilities curve of an economy shifts from AB to CD, it most likely is caused by

(A) full employment of resources.

(B) technology advances.

(C) allocative efficiency.

(D) a decrease in the price level.

(E) productive efficiency.

17. If the production possibilities curve of an economy is CD and the economy is producing at Point X, which of the following is true?

(A) Technology advances changed industrial production.

(B) The quality and quantity of productive resources increased.

(C) Improvements in productivity led to increased output.

(D) Resources are not fully employed.

(E) Aggregate demand decreased.

18. The theory of rational expectations implies which of the following?

(A) Unemployment and the rate of inflation are directly related.

(B) An increase in the money supply will have no effect on price level.

(C) Attempts to decrease unemployment below the natural rate lead to depression.

(D) Attempts to decrease unemployment through government policy will be thwarted by people's reactions.

(E) Government policies work only if the money supply increases by 10 percent.

19. The Phillips curve shows the relationship between

(A) unemployment and economic growth.

(B) unemployment and full employment.

(C) inflation and unemployment.

(D) inflation and investment.

(E) inflation and real interest rates.

20. Which of the following explains why inflation can increase?
I. Increase in aggregate demand
II. Decrease in aggregate supply
III. Increase in rate of money supply growth

(A) I only

(B) II only

(C) III only

(D) I and II only

(E) I, II and III

Sample Short Free-Response Questions

1. Using monetary and fiscal policies, outline an expansionary policy that would encourage long-run growth and explain why the policies will encourage this growth.

2. Some economists want to decrease government spending to reduce government budget deficits. Other economists want to reduce the size of the deficit by raising taxes. Compare these two points of view using aggregate supply and aggregate demand analysis. Illustrate the effects of each program using a correctly labeled aggregate demand (AD) and short-run aggregate supply (SRAS) graph.

3. Why is there a conflict between the Fed's attempts to control both the money supply and the interest rate? What is the implication of the Fed's attempt to control the money supply?

4. Discuss the trade-off between unemployment and inflation in the short run. Why does this trade-off pose a dilemma for policy makers? What trade-off exists between inflation and unemployment in the long run?

5. As the national debt grows, one of the negative effects is crowding-out. Explain the meaning of this term. Identify two sectors of the economy that are involved in this crowding-out. Explain the activities of these two sectors, and show how they interact to create the crowding-out effect. Use a money market or loanable funds market graph to show crowding-out. Use an aggregate demand and aggregate supply graph to show the effects on the economy.

6. Explain the effects on long-term economic growth of using fiscal policy to fight recession and monetary policy to fight inflation.

*7. Using the aggregate supply and aggregate demand model, explain how the use of monetary policy to promote long-run economic growth will affect each of the following:

(A) Short-term interest rates

(B) The composition (mix) of aggregate expenditures

(C) Potential gross domestic product

---

*Actual free-response question from a past AP test. Reprinted by permission of the College Entrance Examination Board, the copyright owner. For limited use by NCEE.

Sample Long Free-Response Questions

*1. Suppose that the following statements describe the current state of an economy:

- The unemployment rate is 5 percent.
- Inflation is at an annual rate of 10 percent.
- The prime interest rate is 11.5 percent.
- The annual growth rate of real gross domestic product is 5 percent.

(A) Identify the major problem(s) the economy faces.

(B) Describe two fiscal policy actions that could be used to alleviate the problem(s). Using the aggregate supply and aggregate demand model, explain how the actions you identified will affect each of the following. Illustrate with a graph.

　(i)　Output and employment

　(ii)　The price level

　(iii)　Nominal interest rates

---

*Actual free-response question from a past AP test. Reprinted by permission of the College Entrance Examination Board, the copyright owner. For limited use by NCEE.

(C) Instead of using fiscal policy to solve the country's problem(s), use only monetary policy. Describe two monetary policy actions that could be used to alleviate the problem(s). Using the aggregate supply and aggregate demand model, explain how the actions you identified would affect each of the following. Illustrate with a graph.

(i)   Nominal interest rates

(ii) Output and employment

(iii) The price level

    Advanced Placement Economics Macroeconomics: Student Activities © Council For Economic Education, New York, N.Y.

*2. Suppose that the following conditions describe the current state of the U.S. economy:

- The unemployment rate is 5 percent.

- Inflation is 2 percent.

- Real gross domestic product is growing at the rate of 3 percent.

(A) First, assume that the federal government increases its spending and increases taxes to maintain a balanced budget. Using aggregate supply and aggregate demand analysis, explain the short-run effects of these policies on each of the following:

   (i)   Output and employment

   (ii) The price level

   (iii) Interest rates

---

*Actual free-response question from a past AP test. Reprinted by permission of the College Entrance Examination Board, the copyright owner. For limited use by NCEE.

(B) Now assume instead that the Federal Reserve buys bonds on the open market. Analyze the impact of this action on each of the following:

(i) Interest rates

(ii) Output and employment

(iii) The price level

(C) Using a graph, analyze the combined effect of the two policy actions described above on each of the following:

(i) Output and employment

(ii) The price level

(iii) Interest rates

3. Suppose that we have two countries: In Country A, the supply of loanable funds is relatively inter-est elastic; and in Country B, the supply of loanable funds is relatively interest inelastic. Assume that both countries are at the same initial equilibrium interest rate and quantity of loanable funds. Suppose that each government implements an expansionary fiscal policy and finances the same size deficit by issuing government securities.

(A) Draw the loanable funds market. Label Country A's supply of loanable funds S_A. Label Country A's new demand curve for loanable funds D_A. Label Country B's supply of loanable funds S_B. Label Country B's new demand for loanable funds D_B. Show the impact of the deficit financing.

(B) If investment in Country A is relatively interest inelastic and investment in Country B is rela-tive interest elastic, explain the impact for each country on each of the following variables:

(i) Investment

(ii) Output

(iii) Price level

(C) Explain in which country crowding-out is greater.

Macroeconomics | Unit 6

International Economics

- People and nations trade to improve their standard of living.

- Because trade is the voluntary exchange of goods and services, the decision to trade will occur only if both parties to the exchange expect to gain from it.

- Voluntary trade promotes economic progress because it allows people and nations to specialize in what they do best.

- The law of comparative advantage explains why there are mutual gains from specialization and trade. Through specialization and trade, nations are able to get beyond, or outside of, their production possibilities curve.

- A nation has an absolute advantage over another nation in the production of a good when it can produce more of that good using the same amount of resources.

- Comparative advantage occurs when a nation can produce a good at a lower opportunity cost than another nation. Relative costs determine comparative advantage.

- Every nation has a comparative advantage in some good or service.

- Trade barriers such as tariffs and quotas limit the potential gains from trade. These barriers generally protect domestic sellers at the expense of domestic buyers. Trade barriers reduce efficiency in the allocation of scarce resources and slow economic progress.

- The balance of payments is a broader measure of international transactions than the balance of trade. The balance of trade considers only a nation's exports and imports of goods, while the balance of payments considers all international economic transactions including the current account, the capital account and official reserves.

- There are three accounts within the balance of payments. The current account records a nation's exports and imports of goods, services, net investment income and net transfers. The capital account records the flows of money from the purchase and sale of real and financial assets domestically and abroad. The official transactions account is an offsetting account for government controls.

- For the current and capital accounts, if foreign currency is used to complete the international transaction, the transaction is a debit (negative). If the transaction earns foreign currency, it is a credit (positive).

- To trade, nations must exchange currencies. An exchange rate is the price of one currency in terms of another and is generally set by supply and demand.

- Appreciation is an increase in the value of a nation's currency in foreign-exchange markets. Appreciation of a nation's currency tends to reduce exports and increase imports.

- Depreciation is a decrease in the value of a nation's currency in foreign-exchange markets. Depreciation of a nation's currency tends to increase exports and reduce imports.

- Monetary and fiscal policies can affect exchange rates, the international balance of trade and the balance of payments.

- Domestic economic policies affect international trade, and international trade affects the domestic economy, influencing economic growth, unemployment and the rate of inflation.

Determining Comparative Advantage

Nations trade on the basis of comparative advantage, but how do we determine who has a comparative advantage? To do this, we need to calculate each country's or person's opportunity costs for both activities. The way we calculate opportunity cost depends crucially on how the productivity data are expressed.

There are two ways to measure productivity: We can calculate output over a given period of time, or we can measure it by the amount of inputs (usually time) necessary to do an activity. Examples of output are tons per acre, miles per gallon, words per minute, apples per tree and televisions produced per hour. Examples of input are number of hours to do a job, number of gallons of paint to paint a house, number of acres to feed a horse and number of pitches to throw a strike. We are going to work through two examples that measure productivity differently.

Part A
Productivity Measures and Example Problems

Output Method

| | Tons Produced per Hour | |
	Fish (A)	Cheese (B)
Ted	60	25
Nancy	45	40

For Ted, the opportunity cost of producing fish in terms of cheese is 60 fish = 25 cheese; therefore 1 fish = $5/12$ cheese. On the other hand, 1 cheese = $12/5$ fish. Similarly we can calculate the opportunity costs for Nancy. We summarize the opportunity cost information in the table below.

	Opportunity Cost (B / A) Fish	Opportunity Cost (A / B) Cheese
Ted	$5/12$ (0.42) cheese	$12/5$ (2.4) fish
Nancy	$8/9$ (0.89) cheese	$9/8$ (1.125) fish

Ted should produce fish because his opportunity cost in terms of cheese is less than Nancy's opportunity cost. Nancy should produce cheese because her opportunity cost in terms of fish is less than Ted's opportunity cost to produce cheese. Ted producing fish and Nancy producing cheese yields the *most* fish and cheese per hour of any combination of production.

Activity written by Jim Charkins, California State University, San Bernardino, Calif. Activity adapted by Jerry De Young, Riverbank High School, Riverbank, Calif., and Ike Brannon, Joint Economic Committee, U.S. Senate, Washington, D.C.

Input Method

Acres Required to Produce One Bushel

	Apples (A)	Pears (B)
Tony	5	2
Chris	6	3

For the input method, the opportunity cost of producing one apple in terms of pears requires that we initially convert the input (acres) into output. For Tony, 5 acres = 1 apple; therefore, 1 acre = $\frac{1}{5}$ apple. Also 2 acres = 1 pear; therefore, 1 acre = $\frac{1}{2}$ pear. Now you can use the same method as for the output method: $\frac{1}{5}$ apple = $\frac{1}{2}$ pear; therefore 1 apple = $\frac{5}{2}$ pear. Likewise 1 pear = $\frac{2}{5}$ apple. We summarize the opportunity costs in the following table.

	Opportunity Cost (B / A) Apples	Opportunity Cost (A / B) Pears
Tony	$\frac{5}{2}$ (2.5) pears	$\frac{2}{5}$ (0.40) apples
Chris	$\frac{6}{3}$ (2) pears	$\frac{3}{6}$ (0.50) apples

Tony has the comparative advantage in producing pears. To produce one bushel of pears, Tony must give up 0.40 bushels of apples, whereas Chris has to give up half (0.50) of a bushel of apples. Thus, the opportunity cost of a bushel of pears is lower for Tony than for Chris, and so Tony should produce pears. Conversely, Chris should produce apples because he has the lower opportunity cost in terms of forgone bushels of pears.

Part B
Practice Problems

First decide whether the problem is an output or input problem; underline *output* or *input*. Then in the space below the table, calculate the opportunity cost of each product and indicate the product with the lower opportunity cost for each person, firm or country. The first one is completed for you.

1. Anna and Barry can grow the following amounts of potatoes and cabbage with the same amount of labor. Type of problem: (*output* / input)

	Potatoes	Cabbage
Anna	100	200
Barry	120	150

For Anna, the opportunity cost of one potato is two cabbages; for Barry, the opportunity cost of one potato is 1.25 cabbages. Barry has to give up fewer cabbages than does Anna to grow one potato. Thus, the opportunity cost of potatoes is lower for Barry than for Anna, so Barry should grow potatoes. Conversely, to grow one cabbage, Anna must give up one-half potato and Barry must give up 0.80 potato. Thus, the opportunity cost of growing cabbages is lower for Anna than it is for Barry, so Anna should grow cabbages.

2. Number caught per day. Type of problem: *(output / input)*

	Deer	Antelope
Henry	4	6
John	24	12

3. Days to produce one unit of each. Type of problem: *(output / input)*

	Cars	Planes
XYZ Corp.	8	10
QKFX Corp.	15	12

4. Acres to produce 100 bushels. Type of problem: *(output / input)*

	Corn	Rice
India	9	3
China	8	2

5. To produce the following from one ton of olives. Type of problem: *(output / input)*

	Cans of Olives	Bottles of Olive Oil
Zaire	60	10
Colombia	24	8

6. Why should a person, firm or country produce the product that has the lower opportunity cost and trade for the other product?

Economic Efficiency and Gains from Trade

The following comparative advantage problems illustrate how two nations can trade even if one is more efficient at producing both products. The country that is more efficient in the production of a good is the country that can produce the good with the least input. In other words, if the United States can produce a ton of oats in three hours and Scotland can produce a ton of oats in four hours, the United States is more efficient in the production of oats. In the language of economics, the United States would have an *absolute advantage* in the production of oats.

A nation has a *comparative advantage* in the good in which it has the lower opportunity cost. The nation should specialize in the good for which it has the lower opportunity cost and trade for the good for which the other country has the lower opportunity cost. A nation with an absolute advantage in the production of both goods will have a comparative advantage in the production of only one of these goods.

Terms of trade is the exchange rate between two commodities, for example, two bananas for 30 grapes. The *gains from trade* are the additional amount of commodities a country has after specialization and trade in comparison with the combination before specialization and trade. For example, a country may gain five bananas relative to the total amount of bananas it had when producing only with its own resources.

Activity written by John Morton, National Council on Economic Education, New York, N.Y.

Underline the correct words in parentheses and complete the questions.

1. The following table gives the number of hours it takes in the United States and Scotland, using the same amount of resources, to produce a ton of oats or one bagpipe.

	Oats	Bagpipe
United States	3 hours	2 hours
Scotland	4 hours	5 hours

(A) *(The United States / Scotland)* has an absolute advantage in the production of oats.

(B) *(The United States / Scotland)* has an absolute advantage in the production of bagpipes.

(C) *(The United States / Scotland)* has a comparative advantage in the production of oats because

(D) *(The United States / Scotland)* has a comparative advantage in the production of bagpipes because

(E) Based only on the data above and comparative advantage considerations, the United States should specialize in *(oats / bagpipes)*.

(F) Based only on the data above and comparative advantage considerations, Scotland should specialize in *(oats / bagpipes)*.

(G) Why will both Scotland and the United States be better off if they specialize and trade?

(H) Suppose that Scotland and the United States agree to specialize according to comparative advantage and to the following terms of trade: 1 ton of oats for 1 bagpipe. In a production period there are 60 hours, and before specialization Scotland produced 7.5 tons of oats and six bagpipes. After specialization and trade with the United States, Scotland wants to maintain the six bagpipes. How many tons of oats will it have? What are its gains from trade?

Advanced Placement Economics Macroeconomics: Student Activities © Council For Economic Education, New York, N.Y.

2. The following table gives the number of hours it takes in the United States and Canada, using the same amount of resources, to produce a ton of wheat or one bolt of cloth.

	Wheat	Cloth
United States	1 hour	2 hours
Canada	3 hours	4 hours

(A) *(The United States / Canada)* has an absolute advantage in the production of wheat.

(B) *(The United States / Canada)* has an absolute advantage in the production of cloth.

(C) *(The United States / Canada)* has a comparative advantage in the production of wheat because

(D) *(The United States / Canada)* has a comparative advantage in the production of cloth because

(E) Based only on the data above and comparative advantage considerations, the United States should specialize in *(wheat / cloth)*

(F) Based only on the data above and comparative advantage considerations, Canada should specialize in *(wheat / cloth)*.

(G) Why will both Canada and the United States be better off if they specialize and trade?

(H) Suppose that Canada and the United States agree to specialize according to comparative advantage and to the following terms of trade: three tons of wheat for two bolts of cloth. In a production period, there are 60 hours; and before specialization, Canada produced nine tons of wheat and 8.25 bolts of cloth. After specialization and trade with the United States, Canada wants to maintain the nine tons of wheat for each production period. How many bolts of cloth will it have? What are its gains from trade?

3. The following table gives the number of hours it takes in the United States and Japan, using the same amount of resources, to produce one computer or one auto.

	Computer	Auto
United States	2 hours	5 hours
Japan	1 hour	4 hours

(A) *(The United States / Japan)* has an absolute advantage in the production of computers.

(B) *(The United States / Japan)* has an absolute advantage in the production of autos.

(C) *(The United States / Japan)* has a comparative advantage in the production of computers because

(D) *(The United States / Japan)* has a comparative advantage in the production of autos because

(E) Based only on the data above and comparative advantage considerations, the United States should specialize in *(computers / autos)*.

(F) Based only on the data above and comparative advantage considerations, Japan should specialize in *(computers/autos)*.

(G) Why will both Japan and the United States be better off if they specialize and trade?

(H) Suppose that Japan and the United States agree to specialize according to comparative advantage and to the following terms of trade: three computers for one auto. In a production period there are 60 hours; and before specialization, Japan produced 40 computers and five autos. After specialization and trade with the United States, Japan wants to maintain the five autos for each production period. How many computers will it have? What are its gains from trade?

Barriers to Trade

The free trade movement started about 200 years ago. Previously, it appears that one of the goals of governments was to stifle international trade, presumably for the benefit of their own economies. Over the last 50 years, there have been efforts to reduce trade barriers, with significant success during the 1990s. Examples of these efforts include the North American Free Trade Agreement (NAFTA), the World Trade Organization (WTO), the European Union (EU) and the Asia-Pacific Economic Cooperation (APEC) forum.

We want to be able to investigate the economic effects of various barriers to trade that a nation might impose to protect domestic industries. In Figure 51.1, the demand curve represents the demand by the domestic economy for a commodity that is produced domestically and also imported. The domestic supply curve indicates what the domestic suppliers are willing and able to produce at alternative prices. If there were no international trade or a complete ban on imports, the equilibrium price would be P, and the equilibrium quantity, Q, would be produced only by domestic firms.

 Figure 51.1
International Trade

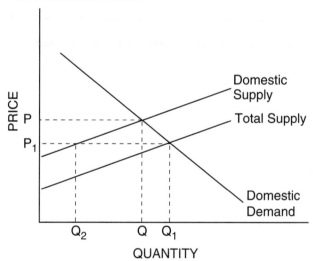

If there is free international trade, the Total Supply curve represents the production by domestic and foreign producers. Domestic consumers would pay P_1 and consume Q_1: They are able to consume more of the commodity at a lower price. Also, at P_1, domestic firms are producing Q_2 and foreign producers are producing $(Q_1 - Q_2)$. Thus, domestic firms are producing less under free trade than they would if the nation did not import the commodity.

Activity written by Rae Jean B. Goodman, U.S. Naval Academy, Annapolis, Md.

Part A
Quotas

Instead of permitting free trade or imposing a complete ban, a nation may decide to set a quota to limit the number of imports. Import quotas are sometimes referred to as *voluntary export restraints* (VERs) because the two countries have agreed that the exporting nation will not export more than a certain amount.

We can see the effect of an import quota by looking at Figure 51.2. Here the domestic price would be P and the quantity would be Q if there were a complete import ban. If there were free trade, the price would be P_1 and the quantity demanded by domestic consumers would be Q_1.

Notice that under free trade, the entire market is supplied by foreign producers as the market is drawn in Figure 51.2. This does not have to be the case; it depends on the costs of the domestic industry and the domestic industry's ability to sell at the lower price.

Suppose the importing nation imposes a quota, or VER, of X amount; the Total Supply with Quota curve represents the new supply curve. Total Supply with Quota is the domestic supply curve plus X amount at every price level ($X = Q_2 - Q_3$). The domestic price has risen from P_1 to P_2, and consumers are able to purchase less of the commodity. Equilibrium quantity has decreased from Q_1 units to Q_2 units. However, domestic producers are now producing Q_3 units, and foreign producers are supplying $X = Q_2 - Q_3$.

 Figure 51.2
Effects of Import Quota

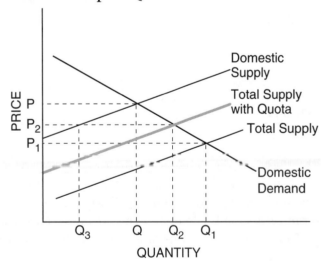

Advanced Placement Economics Macroeconomics: Student Activities © Council For Economic Education, New York, N.Y.

1. Use Figure 51.3 to demonstrate what will happen to the domestic price, domestic production and the amount of imports if a quota is removed. The Domestic Supply and Total Supply curves on the graph are without any barriers to trade imposed. Be sure to show on the graph the supply curve with the quota. It is not on the graph now.

 Figure 51.3
Eliminating a Quota

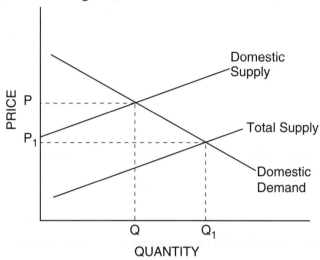

2. Write a paragraph summarizing the advantages and disadvantages of a quota to the domestic economy. Be sure to discuss the impact on domestic consumers, domestic producers and foreign producers.

3. If a quota is imposed, explain the methods people would use to circumvent the effects of the quota.

Advanced Placement Economics Macroeconomics: Student Activities © Council For Economic Education, New York, N.Y.

Part B
Tariffs

A tariff is a tax on an import. The imposition of a tax increases the cost of each unit, which is represented by a decrease in supply. This would result in an increase in equilibrium price and a decrease in equilibrium quantity.

4. Modify Figure 51.4 to show the effect of an import tariff of $T per unit. Be sure to show on the graph the amount of the tariff. Add one curve to the graph, and label it Total Supply with Tariff. After the imposition of the tariff, label the new equilibrium price P_T and the equilibrium quantity Q_T.

Figure 51.4
Effect of Import Tariff

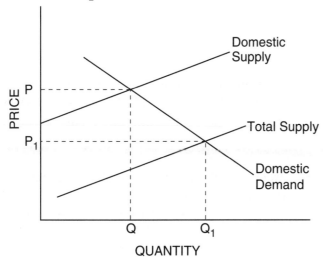

5. What is the effect of the tariff on the equilibrium price and quantity for domestic consumers compared with the free trade levels?

6. What are the similarities between the effects of a quota and those of a tariff?

7. What is the primary difference between the effects of a quota and those of a tariff?

8. Suppose a country can impose either a quota that raises the domestic price to P_2 as in Figure 51.2 or a tariff that raises the domestic price to P_2. Explain whether domestic consumers would prefer a tariff or a quota and why.

Part C
Export Subsidies

Nations may choose to assist domestic industries by providing subsidies to an industry. The subsidies would lower the costs and permit the industry to sell at a lower price. This assistance is called an *export subsidy* because the industry can now compete on the world market and export some of its product to other nations.

9. Modify Figure 51.5 to show the effects of an export subsidy on domestic producers. Indicate as P_S and Q_S the equilibrium price and quantity for domestic consumers after an export subsidy. Add two curves to the graph: a Domestic Supply with Subsidy curve and a Total Supply with Subsidy curve.

 Figure 51.5
Effects of a Subsidy

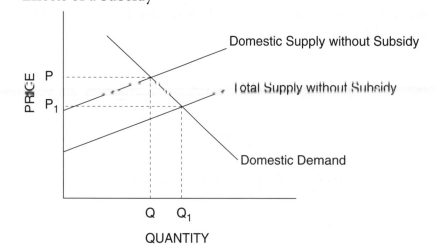

According to Figure 51.5 with your modification, what would be the equilibrium price and quantity for

(A) a completely closed economy (no imports and no subsidy)? _____

(B) an open economy (completely free trade) with no export subsidy? _____

(C) an open economy with a domestic export subsidy? _____

10. What is the effect of an export subsidy on the equilibrium price and quantity for domestic consumers relative to the free trade equilibrium without a subsidy?

11. If an industry receives a subsidy, what will happen at the equilibrium to domestic production and the amount of imports?

Part D
Applications

12. One of the goals of the European Union is the elimination of trade barriers among the member nations. If this goal is achieved, which groups of people will benefit and which will not benefit?

13. Identify the arguments frequently used to impose some type of trade barrier. Discuss the pros and cons of three arguments.

Imbalance of Payments

The place is New York City. The store is McDonald's. A visitor from Japan tries to buy a Big Mac with several yen. The store refuses. McDonald's wants dollars. Somewhere, somehow, this tourist needs to exchange yen for dollars to buy lunch.

The tourist's plight is no different from the situation Boeing faces when it sells airplanes to France. Indeed, whether the product is one Big Mac or 20 airplanes, when people from different nations exchange goods, they also have to exchange currencies. And whether the goods are Big Macs or airplanes, nations like to keep track of currency transactions with other nations. They record purchases of imports, sales of exports, investments in other nations and foreign investment in the domestic country. A record of foreign transactions, called the *balance of payments*, is essential for making sense of a nation's position in the global economy.

There are three accounts within the balance of payments: *current, capital* and *official transactions* (or *reserve*) *accounts*. Market transactions determine the first two; the third is an offsetting account the government controls.

The current account records a nation's exports and imports of goods, services (such as travel to other countries, shipping and insurance), net investment income (U.S. earnings on investment abroad *minus* foreign earnings from capital invested in the U.S.) and net transfers (foreign aid, pensions paid to U.S. citizens living abroad and funds immigrants send to family abroad).

The capital account records the flows of money from the purchase and sale of real and financial assets domestically and abroad. A real asset might be a hotel building in Tokyo, while a financial asset might be shares of stock in a Swedish company. Foreign investors may buy similar assets in the U.S. When these real and financial assets are bought and sold, nations use or earn foreign exchange.

When classifying a transaction, consider whether a country uses (loses) or earns (gains) foreign currency. For the current and capital accounts, if the international transaction *uses* foreign currency to complete the transaction, it is a *debit (negative)*. If it *earns* foreign currency, it is a *credit (positive)*.

The official transactions account is a counterbalancing account: A country uses foreign assets or currency to offset a balance of payments deficit, and this is recorded as a credit (positive). Similarly, when there is a balance of payments surplus, the earned foreign currency is recorded as a debit (negative).

Part A

To make sure you understand the components of the current account, the capital account and the difference between a credit (transaction that earns foreign exchange) and a debit (transaction that uses foreign currency), identify each of the following transactions on the U.S. balance of payments. Complete Figure 52.1 by putting check marks in the appropriate boxes for credit or debit and for capital or current account. The first one has been done for you.

Activity written by Karl Ochi, George Washington High School, San Francisco, Calif.

Figure 52.1
Transactions on the U.S. Balance of Payments

	Credit +	Debit −	Current Account	Capital Account
1. Harley Davidson USA purchases $25 million in production machinery from a Japanese company.		✓		✓
2. André Prenoor, U.S. entrepreneur, invests $50 million to develop a theme park in Malaysia.				
3. A Chinese company sells $1 million worth of berets to the U.S. Army.				
4. BMW pays $1 million to a U.S. shipper for transporting cars from Germany to the United States.				
5. Each month, Ima Grent, who recently arrived in the United States, sends half her paycheck to her sister in Poland.				
6. Bank of America pays $5 million in interest to French depositors.				
7. Senor Ramos from Spain buys a shopping center in Florida.				
8. A Brazilian investor buys five $10,000 U.S. Treasury bonds.				
9. German tourists spend $3 million in the United States; U.S. tourists spend $5 million in Germany.				
10. Brit-Disz, a London record store, spends $10,000 on CDs by the Generic Gurls, a U.S. kiddy-pop group.				
11. Sam Boney, U.S. ice-rink magnate, buys stock in a Chilean ice-rink chain.				

Part B

We can investigate an important balance of payments identity. In the absence of any governmental or central bank intervention, *the current account balance and the capital account balance must sum to zero*. If a nation imports more than it exports (current account deficit), a surplus in the capital account must necessarily offset the deficit because, by definition, goods must either be paid for or the payment is owed. The foreign currency used to buy imports had to come from somewhere (in addition to currency earned from exports); and in this simplified situation, only a capital account surplus could supply the needed foreign currency. In other words, *the excess spending on imports must have found its way back into the United States in the form of foreign investment, a capital account credit.*

12. Analyze the data in Figure 52.2. Compute the missing figures, and answer the questions that follow.

 Figure 52.2

2002 Balance of Payments, Z-Land

Current Account

Z-Land exports of goods	$ +300
Z-Land imports of goods	−400
Z-Land exports of services	+150
Z-Land imports of services	−120
Balance of trade	_____
Net investment income	+10
Net transfers	−14
Balance on current account	_____

Capital Account

Z-Land capital going abroad	−110
Foreign capital coming into Z-Land	+160
Balance on capital account	_____

Balance on Current Account	
Plus Balance on Capital Account	_____

Official Reserves Account

Official reserves transactions balance	_____
Total	$ 0

13. Does Z-Land have a current account deficit or surplus? How do you know?

14. Without central bank intervention, does Z-Land carry a balance of payments surplus or deficit? How do you know?

15. If Z-Land runs a balance of payments deficit, how can this difference be made up? If it carries a balance of payment surplus, what will happen?

Exchange Rates

People, firms and nations exchange products for money and use the money to buy other products or to pay for the use of resources. Within an economy, prices are stated in the domestic currency, such as U.S. dollars or European euros. Buyers use their currency to purchase goods. International markets are different. Producers in other countries who export goods want to be paid in their own currencies so they can carry out transactions. As a result, a *foreign exchange market* develops where national currencies can be exchanged. Such markets serve the need of all international buyers and sellers. The equilibrium prices in these markets are called *exchange rates.* An exchange rate is the rate at which the currency of one nation is exchanged for the currency of another.

Figure 53.1 shows the exchange rates for selected countries for May and August of the same year.

 Figure 53.1
Exchange Rates

	Cost of Foreign Currency in U.S. Dollars (U.S. dollars / foreign currency)		Cost of U.S. Dollar in Foreign Currency (foreign currency / U.S. dollars)	
	May	Aug.	May	Aug.
British pound	1.4	1.8	0.71	0.56
Canadian dollar	0.64	0.63	1.5625	1.5873
European euro	0.87	0.91	1.149	1.099
Swedish krona	0.094	0.093	10.638	10.753
Japanese yen	0.0083	0.0090	120.482	111.111
Mexican peso	0.1101	0.1502	9.083	6.658

Part A

Using the data in Figure 53.1, calculate the cost of the following products in U.S. dollars. To solve, divide the cost of the product in the foreign currency by the cost of the U.S. dollar in the foreign currency.

	May	Aug.
1. A dinner for two that costs 500 Mexican pesos		
2. A hotel room that costs 30,000 Japanese yen		
3. A BMW that costs 85,000 euros in Germany		
4. A pound of Swedish meatballs that costs 30 krona		
5. A pair of pants that costs 72 pounds in London		
6. A leather jacket that costs 1,800 Canadian dollars		

Activity written by Sarah Franklin, Plano Senior High School, Plano, Texas; Nancy Griffin and Ruth Kramp, Plano East Senior High School, Plano, Texas; and James Spellicy, Lowell High School, San Francisco, Calif.

7. Using the exchange table in Figure 53.1, calculate how much foreign tourists would have to pay in their own currency for an American meal that costs $60.00. To solve, divide the cost in U.S. dollars by the cost of the foreign currency in U.S. dollars.

	May	Aug.
British pound		
Canadian dollar		
European euro		
Swedish krona		
Japanese yen		
Mexican peso		

8. Did the value of the dollar appreciate (strengthen) or depreciate (weaken) against the following currencies between May and August? (Put an X in the appropriate column.)

	Appreciate	Depreciate
British pound		
Canadian dollar		
European euro		
Swedish krona		
Japanese yen		
Mexican peso		

Part B

When Americans buy more foreign goods, U.S. dollars are sold in the international currency market to purchase foreign currencies that are used to pay producers in their own domestic currencies. Supply and demand graphs are used to demonstrate such transactions. If the demand for a currency increases, the currency appreciates (strengthens) in value. Currencies sold to purchase other monies depreciate (weaken) in value.

Consider the following situations. In each case, an underlying event causes a change in the supply and demand for currencies. Indicate the impact of each scenario on each currency. The first example is done for you as a model.

9. The prices of U.S. goods rise relative to the prices of German goods.

 Figure 53.2
Prices of U.S. Goods Increase

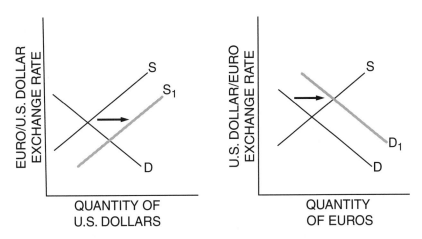

Rationale: *Americans will demand less expensive German goods, thereby increasing the demand for euros and supplying more dollars to the foreign exchange market. The U.S. dollar depreciates. The euro appreciates.*

10. Interest rates in the United States rise faster than interest rates in Canada.

 Figure 53.3
Interest Rates in the United States Increase

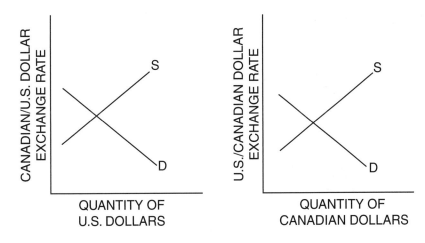

Rationale:

11. French tourists flock to Mexico's beaches.

 Figure 53.4
French Tourists Visit Mexico

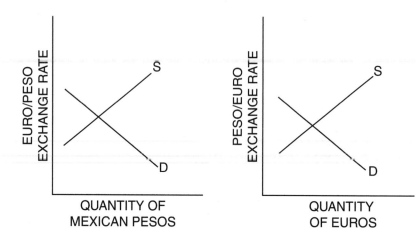

Rationale:

12. Japanese video games become popular with U.S. children.

 Figure 53.5
U.S. Children Want Videos Produced in Japan

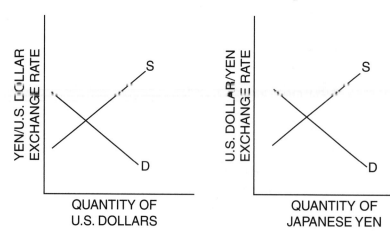

Rationale:

How Monetary and Fiscal Policies Affect Exchange Rates

Changes in a nation's monetary and fiscal policies affect its exchange rates and its balance of trade through the interest rate, income and the price level. Changes in the value of a country's currency may affect the balance of trade and aggregate demand. The value of real output and price levels may also be affected. Domestic policies influence currency values, and currency values influence domestic policies. The complexity of the connection leads to careful evaluation of any change in domestic policy goals. Policy makers cannot ignore the international effects of changes in monetary and fiscal policies.

A series of situations is presented below. In each case:

■ Evaluate the expected effects on exchange rates in the United States and the other country. Use the currency graphs provided to reflect changes in the currency values.

■ Analyze the impact of the currency changes on the U.S. economy as it applies to net exports, balance of trade, aggregate demand and price levels. *Work out the situations in the short run only.*

1. The U.S. government initiates a personal income tax reduction plan, leaving every tax-paying American with more disposable income.

   (A) What will happen as a result to trade between the United States and Taiwan?

* Figure 54.1
U.S. Government Reduces Taxes

Graph A

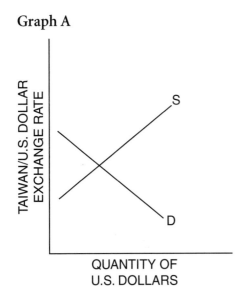

Graph B

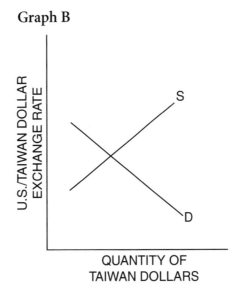

Activity written by James Spellicy, Lowell High School, San Francisco, Calif.

(B) In Graph A, what happens to the U.S. dollar? _____

(C) In Graph B, what happens to the Taiwanese dollar? _____

(D) As a result of the fiscal policy,

    (i)   U.S. aggregate demand shifts (*left / right*).

    (ii) Price levels in the United States (*rise / fall*).

    (iii) U.S. imports *(increase / decrease)*. Explain why.

    (iv) U.S. exports *(increase / decrease)*. Explain why.

2. Japan's fiscal policies lead to an increase in Japan's real GDP.

    (A) What will happen as a result to trade between the United States and Japan?

 Figure 54.2
Japan's Real GDP Increases

Graph A

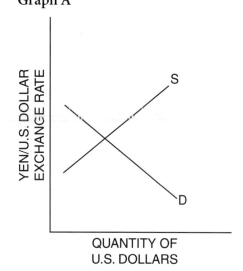

Graph B

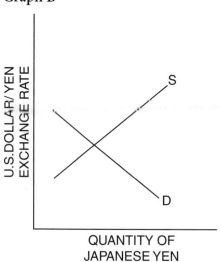

(B) In Graph A, what happens to the U.S. dollar? _____

(C) In Graph B, what happens to the Japanese yen? _____

(D) As a result of the changing value of the U.S. dollar,

    (i)   U.S. exports *(increase / decrease)*. Explain why.

    (ii) U.S. imports *(increase / decrease)*. Explain why.

    (iii) U.S. aggregate demand shifts *(left / right)*.

    (iv) Price levels in the United States *(rise / fall)*.

3. The U.S. federal budget deficit increases, which causes the interest rate to rise. (Assume trade with Great Britain.)

    (A) What will happen as a result to trade between the United States and Great Britain?

✳ Figure 54.3

Interest Rates in the United States Increase

Graph A

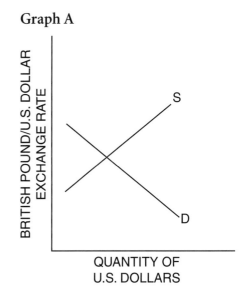

Graph B

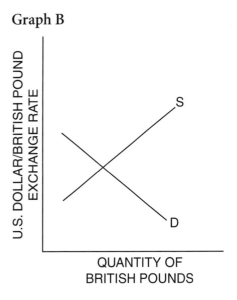

(B) In Graph A, what happens to the U.S. dollar? _____

(C) In Graph B, what happens to the British pound? _____

(D) As a result of the changing value of the U.S. dollar,

    (i)   U.S. exports *(increase / decrease)*. Explain why.

    (ii) U.S. imports *(increase / decrease)*. Explain why.

    (iii) U.S. aggregate demand shifts *(left / right)*.

    (iv) Price levels in the United States *(rise / fall)*.

4. Europe's interest rates are increasing, while the U.S. interest rate remains relatively constant.

    (A) What will happen as a result to trade between the United States and Europe?

✳ Figure 54.4

Interest Rates in Europe Increase

Graph A

Graph B

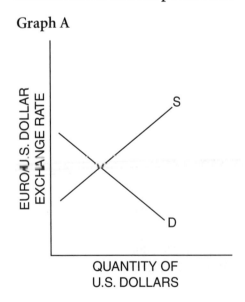

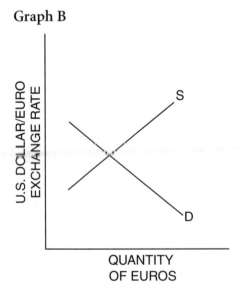

    (B) In Graph A, what happens to the U.S. dollar? _____

    (C) In Graph B, what happens to the European euro? _____

Advanced Placement Economics Macroeconomics: Student Activities © Council For Economic Education, New York, N.Y.

(D) As a result of the changing value of the U.S. dollar,

    (i)   U.S. exports *(increase / decrease)*. Explain why.

    (ii) U.S. imports *(increase / decrease)*. Explain why.

    (iii) U.S. aggregate demand shifts *(left / right)*.

    (iv) Price levels in the United States *(rise / fall)*.

5. There is a rapid increase in the Canadian price level while the U.S. price level remains relatively constant.

    (A) What will happen as a result to trade between the United States and Canada?

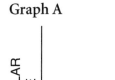 Figure 54.5
The Price Level in Canada Increases

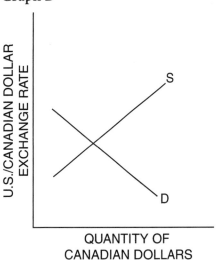

Graph A

Graph B

QUANTITY OF
U.S. DOLLARS

QUANTITY OF
CANADIAN DOLLARS

    (B) In Graph A, what happens to the U.S. dollar? _____

    (C) In Graph B, what happens to the Canadian dollar? _____

(D) As a result of the changing value of the U.S. dollar,

    (i)   U.S. exports *(increase / decrease)*. Explain why.

    (ii) U.S. imports *(increase / decrease)*. Explain why.

    (iii) U.S. aggregate demand shifts *(left / right)*.

    (iv) Price levels in the United States *(rise / fall)*.

The International Way of Thinking

1. True, false or uncertain, and explain why? "Nations do not trade; people trade."

2. Use one example from your own life when you specialized in doing something in which you had a comparative advantage and traded for something in which someone else had a comparative advantage.

3. Assume the U.S. government has placed a high tariff on imported bicycles.

   (A) Use a supply and demand graph to show the effect of the tariff on the U.S. market for bicycles.

(B) Explain the effects of the tariff on the price and quantity of bicycles available to U.S. consumers.

(C) What are the effects of the tariff on

    (i)   foreign bicycle manufacturers?

    (ii) domestic bicycle manufacturers?

    (iii) U.S. consumers?

4. The table below shows how much wine and cheese Germany and France can produce in a day.

	Wine	Cheese
Germany	25 liters	30 kilos
France	50 liters	40 kilos

(A) Which country has an absolute advantage in wine production? Why?

(B) Which country has an absolute advantage in cheese production? Why?

(C) Which country has a comparative advantage in wine production? Why?

(D) Which country has a comparative advantage in cheese production? Why?

(E) Based on the data above and considering comparative advantage only, what should France import? What should France export?

(F) Based on the data above and considering comparative advantage only, what should Germany import? What should Germany export?

5. For each of the following situations, explain the effect of the event on the value of the U.S. dollar in relation to the Mexican peso. Draw a supply and demand graph to illustrate each situation.

(A) Americans increase their demand for Mexican tomatoes.

(B) Inflation in Mexico rises at a higher rate than in the United States.

(C) Americans increase their investments in Mexico because they feel the Mexican economy will be strong.

(D) Interest rates rise in the United States and have become relatively higher than Mexican interest rates.

(E) Mexico becomes a much more popular tourist destination for Americans.

6. Explain three effects of a new law that would forbid U.S. citizens and businesses from trading with any other country.

7. Assume that the United States increases its federal budget deficit, which causes interest rates to rise.

   (A) What would be the effect of this on the international value of the dollar? Why?

   (B) What would be the effect of this on the U.S. balance of trade? Why?

(C) Would the budget deficit and higher interest rates tend to increase or decrease aggregate demand? Why?

8. How could a nation have a negative balance of trade and still not have a deficit in its balance of payments?

Sample Multiple-Choice Questions

Circle the letter of each correct answer.

1. When does the law of comparative advantage indicate that mutually beneficial international trade can take place?

    (A) When tariffs are eliminated

    (B) When relative costs of production differ between nations

    (C) When transportation costs are almost zero

    (D) When a country can produce a product in less time than another country can

    (E) When a country can produce more of some product than other nations can

2. According to the principle of comparative advantage, worldwide output and consumption levels will be highest when goods are produced in nations where which of the following are true?

    (A) Opportunity costs are lowest.

    (B) Absolute advantages are highest.

    (C) The balance of trade is in a surplus.

    (D) The exchange rate is falling.

    (E) The exchange rate is rising.

3. What does a balance of trade deficit imply?

    (A) Exports of goods and services exceed imports of goods and services.

    (B) Imports of goods and services exceed exports of goods and services.

    (C) Investment income received from abroad exceeds investment income paid to foreigners.

    (D) Investment income paid to foreigners exceeds investment income received from abroad.

    (E) Investment by foreigners exceeds domestic investment in other countries.

4. Which of the following transactions represents a deficit in the current account of the U.S. balance of payments?

    (A) The Moscow Capital Investment Corporation makes a loan to a U.S. firm.

    (B) A U.S. subsidiary exports raw materials to its French parent company.

    (C) U.S. firms and individuals receive dividends on U.S. investments in Latin America.

    (D) U.S. tourists in Great Britain purchase pounds sterling.

    (E) Foreigners purchase U.S. securities.

5. An increase in U.S. interest rates relative to the rest of the world can be expected to

    (A) encourage investment spending by U.S. firms in the United States.

    (B) decrease the capital flow into the United States.

    (C) cause a net outflow of foreign capital from the United States.

    (D) increase the international value of the dollar.

    (E) improve the situation for exporters.

6. Which of the following is true if a nation does *not* have an absolute advantage in producing any good or service?

    (A) It cannot have a comparative advantage either.

    (B) It will have a comparative advantage in the production of the good or service in which it has a lower opportunity cost.

    (C) It will export raw materials and import finished products.

    (D) No country will want to trade with this nation because it is not cost effective to do so.

    (E) The international value of its currency will be fixed.

7. Assume a contractionary monetary policy causes interest rates in the United States to increase relative to Japan. In the short run, the value of the U.S. dollar, the value of the Japanese yen and the U.S. balance of trade will most likely change in which of the following ways?

	Dollar	Yen	U.S. Balance of Trade
(A)	Appreciate	Appreciate	Move toward deficit
(B)	Appreciate	Depreciate	Move toward deficit
(C)	Appreciate	Depreciate	Move toward surplus
(D)	Depreciate	Depreciate	Move toward surplus
(E)	No change	Appreciate	Move toward deficit

8. If a nation's currency appreciates, in the short run its net exports and aggregate demand are most likely to change in which of the following ways?

	Net Exports	Aggregate Demand
(A)	Decrease	Decrease
(B)	Decrease	Increase
(C)	Increase	Decrease
(D)	Increase	Increase
(E)	No change	Decrease

9. If exchange rates are allowed to fluctuate freely and the U.S. demand for Japanese yen increases, which of the following will happen?

(A) The U.S. balance of trade deficit will worsen in the long run.

(B) Americans will have to pay more for Japanese goods.

(C) It will be more expensive for the Japanese to buy American real estate.

(D) The dollar will appreciate.

(E) More Americans will want to travel to Japan.

10. If a nation chooses to specialize and trade, which of the following situations could be expected to occur?

(A) Lower prices

(B) Fewer domestic jobs

(C) Decreased resource availability

(D) Decreased dependence on other nations

(E) Decreased quantity and quality of goods

Use the information in the following table to answer questions 11 and 12.

The table below shows the amount of cotton and corn per acre that can be produced in each country with one unit of resources.

	Corn	Cotton
Egypt	400 bushels	500 bushels
Venezuela	300 bushels	200 bushels

11. In the absence of international trade, the opportunity cost of producing one bushel of cotton in Egypt is

(A) 0.8 bushel of corn.

(B) 1 bushel of corn.

(C) 1.25 bushels of corn.

(D) 400 bushels of corn.

(E) Impossible to determine from the information given.

12. If Egypt and Venezuela begin to engage in bilateral trade, then

(A) Egypt will export corn and import cotton.

(B) Egypt will import both corn and cotton.

(C) Egypt will export both corn and cotton.

(D) Egypt will import corn and export cotton.

(E) It is impossible to determine which country will import and export which good .

13. The following data show the quantities of soda and cheese that can be produced in the United States and France with one unit of resources.

	Soda	Cheese
United States	20 bottles	60 pounds
France	10 bottles	40 pounds

Which of the following are true statements?
I. France has an absolute advantage in producing soda.
II. The United States has a comparative advantage in producing soda.
III. The United States has an absolute advantage in producing cheese.
IV. The United States has a comparative advantage in producing cheese.

(A) I only

(B) II only

(C) II and III only

(D) II and IV only

(E) I, II, and III only

14. If the U.S. dollar appreciates in the foreign exchange market, U.S. imports and exports are most likely to change in which of the following ways?

	U.S. Imports	U.S. Exports
(A)	Increase	Remain unchanged
(B)	Increase	Increase
(C)	Increase	Decrease
(D)	Decrease	Remain unchanged
(E)	Decrease	Decrease

15. In the United States, an increase in which of the following will cause an increase in U.S. imports?
I. Per capita real income
II. Price level
III. Interest rates
IV. Tariffs

(A) I and II only

(B) I and III only

(C) I and IV only

(D) I, II, and III only

(E) II, III and IV only

16. The following data show the number of hours it takes in Brazil and Colombia, using one unit of resources, to produce one ton of coffee or one ton of cocoa.

	Coffee	Cocoa
Brazil	5 hours	3 hours
Colombia	6 hours	3 hours

Which of the following statements are true?
I. Brazil has a comparative advantage in producing coffee.
II. Colombia has an absolute advantage in producing coffee.
III. Brazil has an absolute advantage in producing cocoa.
IV. Colombia has a comparative advantage in producing cocoa.

(A) I only

(B) II only

(C) I and II only

(D) I and IV only

(E) I, II and III only

17. Suppose that the price level in Country A increases relative to the price level in other countries. In which of the following ways are Country A's imports and exports most likely to change?

	Country A's Imports	Country A's Exports
(A)	Increase	No change
(B)	Increase	Decrease
(C)	No change	Decrease
(D)	No change	Increase
(E)	Decrease	Increase

18. In the short run, in which of the following ways is an expansionary monetary policy most likely to cause the interest rate and the value of the domestic currency to change?

	Interest Rate	Value of Currency
(A)	Increase	Increase
(B)	Increase	Decrease
(C)	No change	Decrease
(D)	Decrease	Increase
(E)	Decrease	Decrease

19. If interest rates in the United States are increasing faster than interest rates in other countries, which of the following is most likely to occur?

(A) The demand for dollars will decrease, and the value of the dollar will increase.

(B) The demand for dollars will increase, and the value of the dollar will increase.

(C) The supply of dollars will decrease, and the value of the dollar will increase.

(D) The supply of dollars will increase, and the value of the dollar will increase.

(E) The supply of dollars will increase, and the value of the dollar will decrease.

Sample Short Free-Response Questions

1. In a recent year, the United States had a huge balance of trade deficit. Comment on the following policies designed to correct this deficit.

   (A) Limit foreign investment by U.S. firms in other countries.

   (B) Sell dollars so the value of the dollar goes down.

   (C) Put high tariffs on autos, steel and consumer electronics.

2. True, false or uncertain, and explain why? "Tariffs actually increase domestic employment by reducing foreign competition and creating more jobs for American workers. Furthermore, more jobs means higher incomes with which Americans can buy more goods from abroad. Hence, instead of reducing foreign trade, tariffs tend to increase it."

3. Assume that Liechtenstein and Andorra, with equal (and very few) resources, can produce the following:

	Grapes	Wool
Liechtenstein	100,000 kilos	100,000 kilos
Andorra	50,000 kilos	100,000 kilos

(A) Which nation has an absolute advantage in grapes? Why?

(B) Which nation has a comparative advantage in grapes? Why?

(C) Should Liechtenstein specialize in grapes or wool? Why?

(D) Should Andorra specialize in grapes or wool? Why?

4. True, false or uncertain, and explain why? "If a nation has an expansionary fiscal policy and a contractionary monetary policy, the international value of its currency will appreciate."

*5. Assume that labor in the United States becomes more productive because of major technological changes.

(A) Using the aggregate supply and aggregate demand model, explain how the increased productivity will affect each of the following for the United States.

(i) Output

(ii) Price level

(iii) Exports

---

* Actual free-response question from a past AP test. Reprinted by permission of the College Entrance Examination Board, the copyright owner. For limited use by NCEE.

(B) Explain how the change in exports you identified in (iii) will affect the international value of the dollar.

*6. Assume that in the United States, nominal wage rates rise faster than labor productivity. Analyze the short-run effects of this situation on each of the following.

(A) The general price level

(B) The level of exports

(C) The international value of the dollar

---

*Actual free-response question from a past AP test. Reprinted by permission of the College Entrance Examination Board, the copyright owner. For limited use by NCEE.

7. If the rate of inflation is higher in the United States than in other countries, analyze what will happen to

(A) exports

(B) imports

(C) the international value of the dollar

8. Consider a simple model of the world economy in which there are two countries: the United States and Korea. Both produce cars and computers. The labor requirements for producing each good are given in the following table.

	Labor Hours Required	
	Cars	Computers
United States	80	20
Korea	60	10

(A) Which nation has an absolute advantage in producing cars? Explain why.

(B) Which nation has a comparative advantage in producing cars? Explain why.

(C) Show that the nation with the comparative advantage in producing cars can gain from specialization and trade with the other.

Sample Long Free-Response Questions

1. The exchange rate between the Canadian dollar and other currencies has been free to fluctuate since the mid-1960s. For each of the following (in some cases hypothetical) events, indicate whether the value of the Canadian dollar in terms of the U.S. dollar will tend to appreciate, depreciate or remain unchanged. Explain your answer. Use a supply and demand graph to illustrate each situation.

(A) Montreal hosts the Olympics.

(B) The rate of inflation in Canada increases relative to the U.S. inflation rate.

(C) Investors in Quebec purchase substantial real estate in nearby New England and New York.

(D) A consortium of U.S. oil companies constructs a pipeline in Canada to transport natural gas to the United States.

(E) Interest rates rise in the United States relative to interest rates in Canada.

(F) New York and New England utilities contract to buy electricity from Canada's James River hydroelectric facility.

*2. The United States experiences an increase in exports because of changes in the tastes and preferences of foreigners for United States goods. As a result, the following occur:

■ The real gross domestic product rises by 3 percent.

■ The inflation rate rises from 5 percent annually to 10 percent annually.

■ The level of unemployment drops from 7 percent to 5 percent.

(A) Use aggregate demand and supply analysis to explain what has happened in the economy.

(B) Suppose the Federal Reserve decides to sell bonds in the open market. Analyze the short-run effects of this action on each of the following.

    (i)   Interest rates

    (ii) Output and employment

    (iii) Prices

---

* Actual free-response question from a past AP test. Reprinted by permission of the College Entrance Examination Board, the copyright owner. For limited use by NCEE.

(C) Explain the effects of the change in interest rates caused by the Federal Reserve's action in (B) on each of the following.

(i)   The international value of the dollar

(ii) Imports

(iii) Exports

(D) Now the federal government increases taxes while keeping its expenditures unchanged. Analyze the short-run effects of this action on each of the following.

(i)   Output and employment

(ii) Prices

(iii) Interest rates

*3. A series of natural disasters occurs that causes the following changes in the U.S. economy:

- The real gross domestic product drops by 4 percent.

- The inflation rate rises from 5 percent to 10 percent.

- Unemployment increases from 6 percent to 10 percent.

(A) Use aggregate demand and supply analysis to explain what has happened in the economy.

(B) Suppose that the federal government, holding taxes constant, increases its spending and the Federal Reserve increases its purchases of bonds. Explain in detail the short-run effects of these actions on each of the following:

    (i)   Output and employment

    (ii) Prices

    (iii) Interest rate

(C) Explain how exports and imports will be affected by the changes in output and prices resulting from the policies described in (B).

---

4. Suppose the European Union (EU) has decided to impose trade restrictions on agriculture and some specific manufacturing industries. In fact, the EU has decided to subsidize some agricultural products from small farmers and to increase tariffs and quotas on the following key industries: steel, telecommunications, electronics, machine tools, computers and aerospace. The EU hopes these actions will make Europe less dependent on foreign producers for these essential goods.

(A) Which groups will gain and which will lose from these proposed restrictions?

(B) What goals do governments intend to accomplish by imposing trade restrictions?

(C) What are some of the costs that result from trade restrictions?

(D) What would be the likely impact of restrictive trade policies on the total amount of trade between the EU and the rest of the world?

Advanced Placement Economics Macroeconomics: Student Activities © Council For Economic Education, New York, N.Y.

(E) Show graphically how quotas, tariffs and subsidies affect trade.

5. Consider a simple model of the world economy in which there are two nations. The United States produces computers and Mexico produces oil.

(A) Suppose now that the Mexican demand for computers increases while the United States' demand for oil remains unchanged. Use a graph to show what would happen to the value of the Mexican peso.

(B) Explain how the exchange rate changes in a flexible exchange rate system.

(C) Explain how this change in the value of the peso affects Mexico's imports and exports.

Advanced Placement Economics Macroeconomics: Student Activities © Council For Economic Education, New York, N.Y.